The Simplest Sales Strategy

"Every single person on the planet sells ... whether they care to admit it or not! The act of attracting a mate is the perfect example. The guy who gets the girl (or vice versa) is not necessarily the best looking, most intelligent, athletic or most charismatic personality but the one who sells him or herself most effectively. So whether just an average Joe intent on living a happy life or one with aspirations to be a top shot sales professional then my guidance is for you. It provides an easy and quick way of ensuring that you are on top of all situations and promoting yourself to the full. It will help you to win in every selling scenario – professional or otherwise." - JTR

SUCCESSFUL LIVING BY JOSEPH T.RIACH

Mastering The Art Of Making Money

Self-Improvement Should Be Fun!

Winning Big In Life And Business

The Simplest Sales Strategy

NOVELS BY JOSEPH T.RIACH

Too Early For A Glass Of Wine?

RE-WRITE AND EDIT

The Cardboard Suitcase

All available in Paperback and Ebook formats at Amazon (.com and .co.uk), Barnes and Noble and other leading book stores. Contact Tom at www.tomriach.com

THE SIMPLEST SALES STRATEGY

Joseph T.Riach

ISBN : 978-1540678041

© Joseph T.Riach 1998–2019 all rights reserved

All proprietory rights and interest in this publication shall be vested in Joseph T.Riach and all other rights including, but without limitation, patent, registered design, copyright, trademark and service mark, connected with recording this publication shall also be vested in Joseph T.Riach.

Joseph T. Riach

CONTENTS

Introduction

ABOUT THE AUTHOR	1
ABOUT THIS BOOK	3
DEDICATION	5
PROLOGUE	8

The Mindset of a Super Salesman
How to think like a top professional

1. THE MINDSET OF A WINNER	13
2. SCRAPPING IN THE SCHOOL YARD	18
3. FIT FOR SUCCESS	21
4. SPRINTERS COME LAST	26
5. A CONSTANT LEARNER	28
6. ASK A STUPID QUESTION	31
7. WATCH YOUR LANGUAGE	34
8. I WANT	40
9. HOW TO BE SELF-EMPLOYED	46
10. TO RIVAL BRAND POPE	50
11. HOW MUCH HAVE YOU MADE TODAY?	52
12. SELLING AND BUYING	55
13. PUNISHMENT AND REWARD	59
14. A MERC IN THE HAND	61
15. NOTHING PRETENTIOUS	64

The Simplest Sales Strategy
How to close the sale every time!

16. DO YOU WANT IMPULSE BUYERS?	69
17. THE SMARTEST SMOOCHER IN TOWN	71
18. A TRAIN SET NAMED EMOTION	74
19. THE FAG PACK QUOTE	76
20. REPETITION REPETITION REPETITION	78
21. PROFESSIONAL PROSPECT PLAN	83
22. THE ART OF SELLING	91
23. SELLING MADE SIMPLE	97
24. THE SIMPLEST SALES STRATEGY	102
25. CLOSING THE SALE	106
26. THE CREDIBILITY FACTOR	122

The Motivation To Get You To Yes!

IMPOSSIBLE CONVERSATIONS	125
POWER POINTS OF SELLING	135
A WORD FROM THE AUTHOR	142
RESOURCES	145
COPYRIGHT AND DISCLOSURE	150
NOTES AND CONTACT	152

Joseph T.Riach

INTRODUCTION

ABOUT THE AUTHOR

Joseph Tom Riach was born and brought up in the Scottish city of Aberdeen and educated at its famous Grammar School, as indeed was Lord Byron in a previous era.

In young adult life Tom's passion and drive saw him quickly become self-employed and, as a serial entrepreneur, he established, acquired and operated several small businesses. He realised that the success of his enterprises was dependant on the effective promotion and sales of the goods and services he provided and so concentrated his efforts on learning and practicing good sales skills.

Such was his success that in the late eighties, in his freelance roll as a Senior Offshore Investment and Corporate Planning Consultant with major London merchant bank investment arm Hill Samuel Financial Services, he qualified regularly as an international conference delegate and in 1989 became the leading UK producer of new mortgage business.

As a result he was employed by several major companies

to enlighten their sales teams with regard to his success strategies And what he taught them was how to excel in selling through employing the relationship building techniques and knowledge accumulated from his successful endeavours over a thirty year plus career in sales.

It was somewhat inevitable therefore that Tom would in due course turn to writing about his lifetime of sales success in business and finance. He has owned, directed, managed, consulted within and sold within a host of industries and just about any type of business you care to name. Not unnaturally he has amassed an arsenal of knowledge along the way – and not a little wealth!

In a modern world awash with self-styled internet gurus, lifestyle coaches and 'how to' merchants he stands out as one who has actually been there, seen it and done it and, as regards the t-shirt – he probably manufactured it! So when he speaks, it pays to listen.

This is your opportunity, don't waste it.

ABOUT THIS BOOK

These writings first emerged born from my ambition to coach both aspiring and experienced sales people in ways to achieve outstanding results through the application of my simple, easy to learn and employ sales strategies. But I soon realised that my teachings could equally benefit all people regardless of professional ambition or trade, because good sales skills are nothing more than good life skills and practicing good life skills involves regular self-promotion - selling!

The art of selling is little different from many other aspects of life in that it can be a complex activity or it can be a simple one. Many practitioners of sales seem to believe that complexity is not only necessary but that it is also desirable - but they couldn't be further from the truth. The truth is that simple is best and simple works.

Of course the subject of selling is much studied, written of and discussed. Countless books, films and instructional guides have been published and seminars and conventions around the world regularly attract huge audiences, all clamouring to learn the secrets of 'the perfect sale'. And all good professionals should indeed study and seek to learn about selling in depth. Nonetheless it is possible to achieve outstanding results by employing very simple methods.

So this book delivers my 'packaged', easy to understand system which can be employed in any selling environment. It is applicable to any trade or profession and can be practiced in selling any goods or services and in all situations – from the simple retail sale through to complex big ticket contract negotiations … it's a universal solution!

By employing these strategies you will eliminate, both for yourself and the client, all the stress often associated with selling. And with their use it's perfectly possible to enjoy successful selling experiences throughout an entire sales career … and with no real need to understand the process in greater depth. After all, many of the more advanced techniques are already built into the system!

So my book urges followers to concentrate only on providing a rewarding and enlightening experience for your client, then the selling will look after itself.

DEDICATION

This manuscript is dedicated to the professional sales leaders and sales trainers at Hill Samuel Financial Services and Hill Samuel Investment Services, both being arms of the highly respected Hill Samuel merchant bank. These entities no longer exist but my memory of them and gratitude to them is undiminished. They traded in excellence, were quite simply superb at what they did and were the best of the best.

Today I urge both aspiring sales people and those experienced in the profession to do the following :

- Work, train and study to be the very best sales person that you can possibly be

- Work only with those who you trust implicitly, can look up to and learn from

- Sell only the finest product or service, one in which you have total belief and confidence

- Represent only a company which provides the highest quality product or service

- Represent only a company which provides the highest

quality training, support and back up

- Represent a company which pays the highest commissions and does so timeously and without quibble

- Represent a company and work only with people of integrity

Finding a host company which satisfies just two or three of those criteria may well be difficult. More so to find one which satisfies them all. But don't be discouraged. Hill Samuel was such an entity. The company consisted of people who, from the top down, were endowed with the highest ethical and professional standards. The result of which was that they created a centre of excellence to which they could bring the brightest and best talent in the land.

I owe them a huge debt of gratitude. Much of what I became, achieved and what I am today is down to the schooling I received from them and the example in excellence which they set. If you are intent on gaining success in any trade or profession and in any discipline, not just sales, then aim to uphold the Hill Samuel ideals, ethics and standards.

Doing so will not just make you a more successful, wealthier sales or business person ... doing so will raise to unimaginable heights your own self-esteem and the regard in which others hold you.

Joseph 'Tom' Riach

PROLOGUE

This book is all about selling. Naturally the focus is on learning the skills of professional and ethical sales practices. But never overlook the importance of your own spiritual and physical well-being. These two are far, far more important than mere monetary or material gain. Without them you are nothing. So attend to them. Make spiritual wealth the bedrock, and physical well-being the cornerstone, of your existence. With these in place and functioning then success in other areas of your life becomes virtually guaranteed.

In my book there are *Three Simple Steps* it is necessary to follow in order to *become a professional sales person of the highest order*. These are :

1. Adopting the mindset of a super salesman - focussed, client orientated and *smart*.

2. Learning and employing one simple selling strategy to guarantee success in all sales situations.

3. Working progressively to increase knowledge, improve technique and embrace the third level solutions in

the selling process.

There is of course, no short cut to success but there IS an art to successful selling. Few possess this skill and fewer still wish to share their knowledge ... but by altering the way you think of selling and by paying heed to some simple but often unspoken of strategies referred to in these pages, you may well come to master the art!

Unlimited wealth through selling is here within your grasp.

Go for it!

Joseph T. Riach

BOOK 1

THE MINDSET OF A SUPER SALESMAN

How To Think Like A Top Professional

Joseph T.Riach

Chapter 1

THE MINDSET OF A WINNER

Those who wish to work in sales and intend to be among the most successful, highest earners, first need to embrace one stark reality. You are going to have to work in a distinctive way and adopt an attitude, a mindset which is totally different from the vast majority of the population.

If, for example, your idea of becoming wealthy is to win the lottery, then read no further. This book is not for you. On the other hand, if you believe that it is possible for you to learn to 'think successful' and then become successful, then read on. Successful sales people in terms of wealth know that the odds in favour of a certain combination of numbered balls falling in their favour are so miniscule as to be NIL. They will not therefore waste any of their precious life time on such useless daydreaming. It is a fact that only a tiny percentage of wealthy people have their fortunes given to them, whether by lottery win, inheritance or whatever. The vast bulk of wealthy people create their own fortune. This is never more true than with top sales professionals.

POWER POINT – *"Top sales professionals CREATE their own* *fortune."*

They realise from the outset that if they utilise their own abilities, simply and consistently then the odds of achieving success and wealth swing dramatically in their favour. In fact, they believe that when a person takes full control of their situation and assumes full responsibility for all of their actions, then success becomes a virtual certainty!

POWER POINT - *"When you take full control of your situation and assume full responsibility for all of your actions, success becomes a virtual certainty."*

But to 'think successful' takes a certain mindset. And, given that only a very small percentage of people are 'successful' and wealthy – 5% no more – it follows that only this select group have the 'right' attitude in this context. Therefore it also follows that everyone else's attitude in this context is the 'wrong' attitude. Now this is a very important point indeed. It means that the opinions and ideas with regard to financial success of Ninety Five Per Cent of the population, as espoused daily on television, in the pub and in the workplace are totally worthless. They may make up 95% of opinion but *they **make up 100% of unsuccessful opinion**! The ideas and practices of the Five Per Cent on the other hand – **make up 100% of successful, entrepreneurial*** *opinion. And these very success ideas and practices will be totally alien to what the other 95% (Joe Public) thinks contributes to success.*

POWER POINT – *"Learn to think like the wealthy 5% and accept that you will be different from 'Joe Public'."*

The first and most important difference with the successful few is their mindset, their attitude. Many in the wider population think that success is down to luck. We'll ignore that. Most of the rest consider that wealthy winners are possibly cleverer than them in some way or perhaps that they 'cheat'. Therefore they look for the 'secrets' of wealth and the wealthy in ever more complex areas. Yet the very opposite is the truth. Very successful people generally follow very simple wealth creation practices. So simple in fact that the majority of people cannot see or will not believe that these practices lie at the very heart of their success.

It's somewhat like the clue to the murder sitting on the mantelpiece. No-one expects it to be there, so no-one finds it. They search every nook and cranny, upturn every stone. To no avail. Yet all the time the answer is right there before their eyes. So with success and wealth. It is simple activities carried out repetitively and well which mount up to great achievements. This is the single most powerful 'secret' of super successful sales people !

POWER POINT – *"Simple activities carried out repetitively and well are what mount up to great achievements."*

But this is what so many people cannot or will not see. So, before you can become a top professional salesman, it will be necessary for you to learn to think the way that they do. This will usually involve a process of *UNeducating* from your mind many well entrenched beliefs and practices.

POWER POINT – *"Learning to act simply will not be easy. Be prepared to uneducate yourself from thinking and working in complex ways."*

As very young children we mostly all display a high level of native wit. A range of natural thought processes and actions designed to allow us to live successfully in the wild. But modern society sanitises out much of this through our culture and education. So, by the time most people reach their twenties, they have totally capitulated to the expectations of society and to the peer pressure of 'the herd'. They are thinking and acting just like all the other average Joes who display, in all their thoughts and actions, a desperate desire to be equal in mediocrity.

POWER POINT – *"The majority of the population display by* *all their thoughts and actions a desperate desire to be equal in mediocrity."*

Elite sales people on the other hand want to be over-achievers and are prepared to DO something different in order to improve their lot. Most evolve a remarkably simple plan of action and then repeat it over and over again. They work to develop the mindset of a winner!

Chapter 2

SCRAPPING IN THE SCHOOL YARD

Scrapping in the school yard was an almost daily occurence in the early teen years of my youth. Some lads were of course more active in this department of extra curricular activity than others but most got into a brawl with a class mate at some time or another. The fights were more part of the necessary rite of passage to manhood rather than anything more sinister but, nevertheless, they could be brutal. And like any area of life or any activity, some participants were simply better at it than others.

Given my ringside view and frequent personal involvement in these skirmishes I arrived at conclusions regarding the superiority of the regular winners which would, in the same tradition as that of many childhood games, stand me in good stead in later life. Other than learning the rather obvious negative health benefits of broken noses and cracked teeth, I learned these three critical lessons :

The first was that winning had little to do with size or strength or even technique. But had everything to do with attitude!

The second was that winners invariably struck first. They didn't hang around and give the initiative to their opponent.

And the third was that winners chose their fights carefully, only venturing into conflict when certain of success.

I have adopted and practiced all three of these 'attributes' throughout my life and sales career. There is no doubt in my mind that they have been central to my success. Let's look a little more closely at their significance.

Attitude : Being assertive, self-confident, unflinching and totally committed. When you deeply believe in your own invincibility and display that with courage and conviction then few can stand against you. The opposition is beaten before they even square up.

Strike first : Several popular expressions come to mind – 'Fortune favours the brave' … 'Time and tide wait for no man' … 'Let others wait and wonder' and my own favourite maxim which I've quoted and practiced many times over the years – 'Possession is nine points of the law'. In other words act and take control, establish a position of strength first and let others argue later if they wish, but from a position of weakness. The first blow is most often the decisive one.

Pick your fights : Winners fight only when certain of success and thus develop a reputation as ... winners! This then snowballs and becomes self-fulfilling. Once seen as winners then they generally are. Additionally, by not competing when unsure of victory they open the door to negotiation and compromise from which all parties may benefit without conflict or hostility. Plus they can defer a punch-up to a later time when they can be in position to be sure of victory.

Yes scrapping in the school yard is to school what the drinks parties are to a business convention ... the place where the real action is and an awesome training ground.

POWER POINT - *"Winners are mentally tough, strike early and choose their moments well."*

Chapter 3

FIT FOR SUCCESS

I have always been one of those lucky people who can eat as much of whatever I want yet stay as slim as a pencil. Of course I make my own 'luck' too. As a kid I was the exact opposite of todays desk-shackled computer generation, I was forever on the move. I ran everywhere. I'd run the mile to school and back each day, play endless football matches in the school yard, climb and hike in the mountains and swim in the sea. Then there were physical training periods at school, games days, the athletics club and gymnastics, more football, rugby, cross country runs and the swimming and life saving clubs. Life was a blur of constant action.

My first real organised training sessions started with the school rugby team when I was twelve years old then picked up pace at fourteen when I started to play for my first youth football club. Since then, give or take the odd break, I have trained every day of my life. At my peak I was training rigourously for two hours twice per day and was as fit as any Olympic athlete. Today things have slowed somewhat but I still exercise most days.

As a lifelong business entrepreneuer were I to be asked how I define myself, I'd answer, "As an athlete first and a businessman second." You see, like many other aspiring athletes, when success and the prospect of a sustainable income-producing career in sport didn't materialise, I redirected my energy into business, specialising particularly in sales. The selling arena is a tough one. A competitive, even cut-throat environment, demanding effort and dedication. Only the most resolute prevail. It thus goes a long way to satisfying the competitive instincts of a frustrated sportsman.

POWER POINT - *"The world of selling is tough and competitive, demanding effort and dedication. Only the most resolute prevail."*

So if you're going to be in sales it's as well to be physically fit. Fitness will sharpen your performance all round, raise your awareness and intensify your thought process.

Of course we all know of or have encountered hugely successful entrepreneurs, business leaders and sales professionals who are grossly overweight or heavy smokers or who never exercise – who are anything but fit. This would suggest that physical fitness is not a necessary prerequisite to success. But to those who are of that view I'd simply say, "Imagine what such people could have achieved had they been fit too!" I have written elsewhere that, *"There is nothing you do in life that you won't do better through reading a book."* I'd add to that that there is nothing that you do in life which you won't do better by being physically fit.

POWER POINT - *"There is nothing that you do in life which you won't do better by being physically fit."*

I read recently of a multi-million dollar research programme having been completed by doctors at a leading university in which they concluded that physical exercise improves memory retention. My reaction was one of amusement. The (famous) phrase, "I could have told them that!" came to my mind. And I could have told them that (and at considerably less expense)! because I know from my own experience that my physical exercise not only keeps my body in shape, it keeps my mind toned too. The two work in tandem, they feed each other. Constant training, day in and day out takes will and determination. That comes from the mind. But the exercise itself sends oxygen, nutrients and cleansing agents around all of the body including the brain and thus keeps it sharp and in good working order. So physical training is brain training and vice versa. It's win-win!

POWER POINT - *"When you exercise your body, you*

exercise your mind and vice versa. It's win-win!"

In addition I actively practice brain exercises. Simple things like running through my multiplication tables first thing in the morning when I awaken to the more complex research and authorship projects I undertake. Any work involving active brain usage is in fact brain exercise. Writing this material is one …..

As success is something that we all strive for, whether in small ways or as in major achievements, it's important to recognise that successful sales people generally employ a very simple plan of action which they repeat over and over. In fact, simple activities carried out repetitively and well are what mount up to great achievements.

POWER POINT - *"Simple activities carried out repetitively and well are what mount up to great achievements."*

Daily exercise is itself a simple, repetitive act. It instils confidence and self belief as well as invigorating the body and mind. It should be an important part of your life success plan.

Are you fit for success?

Footnote : When you consciously blend mental exercise into your physical training sessions you can also be practicing good time management! For example, if you recite your favourite motivational mantras (eg 'Every day in every way I'm getting better and better') or listen to them on your MP3-Player while jogging you will not need to set aside separate time for repeating them later – and you can pack a heck of a lot of repetitions into a one hour training run! And sales ideas, projects, speeches and scripts can all be worked on and developed while you work out.

Chapter 4

SPRINTERS COME LAST

I love watching sprinters in action. Rippling muscles and explosive power. They're not at all like distance runners or grand tour cyclists who tend to be lean, wiry and built for endurance.

But of the two, sprinters and long distance athletes, it is the latter who are closer to possessing the physical characteristics of the human race in general.

Man in fact owes his pre-eminence over all other creatures in the world to just that, his ability to keep going over long periods of time and therefore able to succeed as a hunter and chase down far faster prey. So that same stamina is in our DNA, everyone possesses it. It gives us the strength required in order to succeed in life or business. It's often referred to as staying power.

Sprinters, in business terms, are the 'white suits and gold Rolls Royce and Rolex brigade', all show, here today and gone tomorrow. Really successful people are by comparison in it for the long haul. You should be too!

POWER POINT – *"You sprint for show but you jog for dough!"*

Chapter 5

A CONSTANT LEARNER

Learning is a natural process which starts from the moment we are born. We are all throughout life constant learners. But some learn better than others and as we progress through life the act of acquiring knowledge and skills becomes a much more pro-active pursuit rather than being just a natural phenomenon. So those who work at being a constant learner and who strive to always add to their learning, their knowledge and their abilities can develop an advantage over those less inclined to work on self improvement in this way.

Yet learning itself is not enough in terms of being successful in life or business. Knowledge is of little value if not put to use. For those who possess the talent to teach, utilising knowledge can entail simply passing on the knowledge learned or acquired to others and there is value in that. But not if at every turn the student simply becomes a teacher and then passes on the learning to the next student and so on and so on ad infinitum, without ever having applied the knowledge or practised the skill inherent in it.

Then clearly nothing of value is ever produced and the perpetual promotion of the knowledge is purely academic and not financially sustainable.

This, for example, is what happens with much present day internet marketing. There is no product and no service other than the endless passing on of the same advice from one person to another, none of whom have any actual experience of doing the thing which the advice pertains too! A totally futile exercise.

On the other hand, where real knowledge is applied in a productive way to an active endeavour or to an enterprise then true value, income, profit can be created. Plus, one who has both learned and then applied the knowledge or skill successfully will in the process have acquired actual experience in the doing of it and that will be of genuine value, theoretical and practical, when later teaching or encouraging others. And that's the only really meaningful knowledge worthy of receipt, possession of or transfer to others.

So understand that working at what you do is in itself educational (often called experience) and necessary but it is wise to accelerate and supplement your learning through ongoing professional training and scholastic studies too. And mix with and learn from your peers, those experienced in life generally and in your particular areas of speciality and enterprise.

The pay off is that it's the surest way to make certain that you always earn, and earn well, in your chosen trade or profession.

POWER POINT - *"A constant learner is a constant earner!"*

Chapter 6

ASK A STUPID QUESTION

Was there a pupil in your form at school who the rest of the class laughed at for regularly asking what they perceived to be silly questions? That pupil was me.

Then in later years at college, night school or adult education was there also that one inevitable student capable of reducing the class to hysterical laughter with what were apparently equally stupid questions? That was me too.

And had you been a member of my profession in my early years in its ranks, or the proverbial fly on the wall, then there in the front row at conferences, seminars and training schools you'd likewise find me firing off my salvo of questions weird and bizarre, to the perplexion of the speakers and the entertainment of all.

Myself and my colleague Duncan (he being similarly endowed with lateral thinking inquisitiveness – there's few of us about)! had learned that we could show at the last minute to these events because our seats in the front row were assured by the fact that venues tended to fill from the back rows forward. Plus, in many instances, our front row seats were kept for us by those intent on ensuring a good laugh! So, one way or another, we were always best placed to easily interrupt presentations and harangue speakers with our 'stupid' questions.

But as our 'notoriety' spread, over time so did its nature. We had you see grown to become two of the most prolific producers of new business in the industry. So whereas previously our questions had been greeted with guffaws and the rolling of eyes, now when we interrupted and rose to speak an attentive silence descended. Delegates leaned forward to better hear what was being queried. The mood had become one of – what rich wisdom is in the question?

POWER POINT – *"Top sales people are questioners and listeners – not talkers."*

So without being aware of it our audiences had themselves become by association askers of stupid questions! Somewhere in the collective conscious had been seeded the realisation that being bright, educated, intellectual even, wasn't bringing wealth or success. But that an enquiring mind and a desire to know, even to the point of appearing stupid to your peers, was what produced results.

Inevitably therefore, both Duncan and myself in time found a constant stream of inquirers seeking us out, each one primed with the same hopeless question of the inspirationally lame – "What is the secret of your success?"

Of course we had a ready answer – "Ask a stupid question!"

POWER POINT – *"Asking 'stupid' questions is smarter by far than not knowing."*

Chapter 7

WATCH YOUR LANGUAGE

There are certain words and expressions which successful sales people never, but never use. They don't even think them. They have eradicated from their conscience, and sub-conscience, all reference to them. Why? Because it is your duty as a sales professional, both to yourself and to your clients, to be positive and upbeat in all that you say and do. It is your job to be optimistic.

Those people who do use the words and expressions which I am about to comment on immediately expose negative vibes whenever and where-ever they speak or communicate. They identify themselves as the average, typical no-hoper.

So if you have ever used in the past, or indeed do use now, any of the following then, if you are really serious about creating success and growing to becoming a professional sales leader, one looked up to and respected by all, then resolve from this very minute to never ever even think these words let alone utter them. Eradicate all memory of, and reference to them – now! Because negative thoughts become negative words become negative actions.

POWER POINT - *"Negative thoughts become negative words become negative actions. Eradicate from your mind all reference to them."*

My list is not exhaustive, there are many more, but here are the four expressions in everyday use which I find the most abhorrent – I can barely bring myself to write them :

1. "It's not fair." – 'Fair' is without doubt the single most abhorrent word. The expression, "It's not fair," is typically used by sad, round-shouldered, whinging gits! Get this straight – there is no such thing as 'fair'. The world was not created 'fair'. Life is not 'fair'. 'Fair' is a non-existent comparative measure, it's totally meaningless, useless. The use of this four letter 'F' word implies that the person expressing it believes that he or she bears no responsibility at all for their lot in life, their own actions and their lack of good fortune but that everyone and anyone else is somehow responsible for them and is to blame. It's use betrays negativity, naivety and a dreadful attitude. It goes hand in hand with the blame culture rife in present day society. So much easier to hold someone else to account rather than take a good, hard look at ones self.

POWER POINT - *"The word 'fair' is meaningless. It's a far* *more obscene and less desireable expression than the other four letter 'F' word in common use!"*

Unfortunately, we hear the 'fair' word in all too common use. And it's not just by seven year olds in the playground complaining because their lollipop is smaller than their friends one! No, you'll hear it in the media, on TV and often used by politicians. Many of the last mentioned know full well of course that there is no such thing as 'fair' but they use the term for their own purposes, as a weapon, as a means of turning attention from themselves or on to an adversary or a particular group in society. In simple terms it suits politicians (and some others) to have the populace at large believe that 'fair' exists. But it doesn't.

What does exist however for those in touch with the real world are the words 'Equitable' and 'Just'. These words have entirely quantifiable meanings and therefore, appropriate applications. They belong firmly in the vocabulary and thoughts of right-minded people. Top sales people do use these words. So too should you.

POWER POINT – *"The words 'Equitable' and 'Just' are real words with real meaning. Think simple, think clearly, use real words and expressions."*

2. "It's not my fault." – Generally means that it is! Successful sales people accept full responsibility for their own actions, all their own actions. They know that they alone create entirely the life that is theirs. They never subscribe to the mistaken belief that our lives are somehow forced upon us or are created for us by others. They believe in self-determination and freedom of thought and expression. The first place that sales professionals always look when questioning events affecting them is – in the mirror!! Their ability to be self-critical and analytical is one of their great strengths.

POWER POINT - *"The ability of top sales professionals to be sef-critical is one of their great strengths. When questioning events affecting them they look first, in the mirror."*

This is what taking responsibility is all about, not blaming someone else. "It's not my fault", is a cop out, an abdication of responsibility and, yes, it's childish. It denies the simple truth that almost any event that may occur to us at any time, anywhere in our lives, our businesses, our relationships is brought about or triggered by our own actions. But when a salesman takes it upon himself to be responsible for himself, for his life, for his situation and for all of his thoughts and deeds, then he has taken the first and most important step towards achieving great things. Let lesser mortals whinge and watch in awe!

POWER POINT - *"When you take it upon yourself to be responsible for yourself, for your life and for your situation then you take the first step to achieving great things."*

3. "Problem." - The word 'problem' I never use, yet it crops up all the time. To me it is a negative word, it implies worry. Such as "I have a problem at work" or "I've got money problems" etc. To so many people life is just a series of never ending problems. But to successful sales professionals, the idea of a 'problem' doesn't exist! They speak instead of 'situations'. And they recognise life as simply a series of evolving situations. Each one a challenge demanding action yes, but which, when resolved, leads to the next situation – and so on. Viewed thus, there are no 'problems' - and therefore nothing to worry about! There is no stress or conflict in life as being in a situation is the normal state of being. So think positive. Talk only situations!

4. "I'm bored." - Is an expression which, when I hear it, not only makes me angry but also fills me with disbelief. I just cannot comprehend how any remotely intelligent being could ever be bored. In fact I point-blank refuse to acknowledge the existence of the state of boredom. As a kid I was the exact opposite of todays desk-shackled computer generation, I was forever on the move Life was a blur of constant action and remains so to this day. There simply are not enough hours in a day, days in a week, weeks in a year or years in a lifetime for me to do everything that needs doing and all the things I want to achieve ... but I have a damned good try! Those who claim boredom are just not trying. If they looked they'd find plenty to do, if not for themselves then for others. Put it this way ... How could anyone be bored when there are so many people out there needing help? The old, the sick, the lonely and the disadvantaged. To anyone who says they're bored, I say, "Find someone less fortunate than yourself to help and give of your time to them. And when you do that you'll find that not only are your days filled but you yourself will be fulfilled. There will simply be no place in your life for boredom!"

Chapter 8

I WANT

You may well have heard this before but make no mistake, following is one of the most important pieces of information regarding achieving success in sales, or any other pursuit, that you will ever receive. It is fundamental to success. So I make no apologies for repeating the advice – *"Whenever you have an idea or an ambition to really achieve something then you **must** start by putting in writing your intention."* If you haven't heard that before then take note now!

POWER POINT – *"Whenever you have an idea or an ambition to really achieve something then you must start by putting it down in writing."*

You see an idea is only an idea and nothing more while it is in your head. On that premise ideas are worthless. Everyone has great ideas but only a handful of people ever get round to actually putting their ideas into practice. And the first requirement in turning an idea into reality, is to write it down! Then the thought starts to become tangible, to be real. That's why, for instance, if you go to your bank to request finance for your proposed venture the first thing that you'll be asked for is your business plan. The bank knows that everyone and Tom Cobbly has ideas but what they want to see is that you are made of the right material to turn your idea into reality. Thus they need to know that in the first place you can turn your idea into a written plan. If you can do that then there's a better likelihood that you can also go from plan to implementation.

POWER POINT - *"Turning an idea into a written plan is the first necessary step to make in progressing from an idea to implementation."*

My first sales ventures lacked a written or any real plan, therefore were doomed to failure. Later I planned well, documented and laid out my proposals and intentions clearly and, as a result, achieved great things. But over time, although I achieved, I found that I didn't always get the material nor the spiritual rewards which I truly wanted from the venture.

And in due course I came to realise why this was so. What I discovered changed not only my attitude to planning and writing down my ideas but also my whole view of why I was in sales in the first place. As with most issues in life, the revelation was incredibly simple – there's that word 'simple' again!

What I realised was this – None of my plans included as part of the plan, a list of material or spiritual things and lifestyle requirements which I wanted to gain from the venture. I'm not refering to generalities like *'success'* or *'lots of money'*, these are far too vague. I mean specifics like *'one million dollars in the bank'* or *'a brand new Mercedes top range coupe in midnight blue with beige leather interior'* or *'I want to work only three days a week, have no employees, own a villa in the Caribbean where I live three months in the year'* or *'I want to work only with those to whom their word is their bond and for whom their integrity is their most valued asset'* – Get my point? Not only that but I realised that my 'I Want' list had to be the start point of the whole plan, the reason for the plan's existence.

POWER POINT - ***"Before writing your sales business plan, start by writing down your 'I Want' list of material objects and lifestyle requirements which the venture is intended to create for you."***

So now, whenever I draw up a sales or business plan, I start with the specific material possessions and/or lifestyle requirements which I intend to create from the venture. Then I design the venture around these wants and shape it in order that my wants will be realised. In other words, I've made my wants the raison d'etre of the whole plan. They are the only reason the plan exists. And why not? Why would I set up a sales project which led me into a life of doing something which I didn't want to do, made me unhappy and provided none of the things, material or spiritual, which I wanted from life? Answer – I wouldn't. Yet many people do precisely that. I've encountered countless sales people in my life who are working endless hours in work they don't enjoy, suffering poor quality family life and leisure time, have little or no savings and few of the possessions they'd love to own. And why? Because they didn't start off with, write down and stick with a business plan based 100% on the 'I Want' principal.

By comparison, when my sales plans are put into practice, they function with the sole intention of providing me with my wants. In that way, I get from the project those pre-determined wants – no more, no less. Result, one very happy me.

There is another important aspect to writing sales plans based on the 'I Want' principal. Simply it's this – It is almost certain that to become a top earning sales professional, you will have to be self-employed and earning by way of commission. This is virtually a 'must'. Because only when working for yourself do you have sole and total control of your own life and events in it. Only in this circumstance can you be independently responsible for all you create and what you achieve. In this state your prospects become unlimited, unfettered by outside restraints.

POWER POINT - *"Take control of your own destiny and accept responsibility for all that happens to you by becoming your own boss."*

Only when thus in control of your own destiny are you in a position to turn your ideas for success into sales plans and then into actual projects based on your 'I Wants.' And without an 'I Want' starting point to the sales plan, there is no full control of your situation. And, as we've seen, those without an 'I Want' base to their plans will not achieve from their projects those real things – material, lifestyle and spiritual – which they'd actually wish to. So, in order to achieve success in the sales world, you really need to be your own boss, write a sales plan and base the plan on your 'I Want' list.' Simple really, isn't it?

POWER POINT - *"You must become your own boss and write down your business plan based on your 'I Want' list."*

So remember, only when your 'I Want' list has been

comprehensively detailed should the actual sales plan be created. From the written plan will evolve eventually the venture or project; the project will be progressed and at regular points (eg year ends) will have conclusions. And having achieved the successful completion of the project then you reward yourself with your wants exactly as was detailed in your 'I Want' list – Drives off into the sunset in Midnight Blue Mercedes top range coupe, happy and smiling!

I can vouch wholeheartedly for the effectiveness of the 'I Want' approach. Writing down a proper plan will achieve success where it just cannot be possible without a plan. But when your plan incorporates at its core the 'I Want' strategy then it becomes totally focussed and dynamic. It delivers the goods exactly as you predetermine and, on that basis, has a significantly greater success rate than plans not based on 'I Want.' 'I Want' provides complete satisfaction. Try it and see!

Chapter 9

HOW TO BE SELF-EMPLOYED

As a self-employed sales person I have always viewed my business as consisting of *three of Me* :

Me 1 is the owner or shareholder of the business. I set up the business as an investment for Me and to provide Me with income.

Me 2 is the MD of the company. My role is to ensure the business runs effectively and profitably. I am answerable to the shareholder and responsible for over-seeing all operational aspects of the business, including -

Me 3 who is the sole employee of the company. I am responsible for day to day work and activity within the business. I answer to **Me 2**, the MD.

When **Me 2** does his job well he will ensure that the business remains healthy and he will motivate and support **Me 3**, including ensuring that discipline within the business is maintained eg. good time-keeping, impeccable standard of work, meticulous financial management, no waste - and no pilfering!

The Simplest Sales Strategy

So, in simple terms, when the business is healthy it will be able to provide **Me 1** with a good investment and regular income. I look after the business, it looks after me!

If I don't look after the business well? ... then all three of me are stuffed!

This approach to practicing the management of sales agent self-employment in this manner is of course no different to the standard model which governs the successful stewardship of almost any business. An investor in the open market would want to invest in a sound company. That is a company which is :

- *Well established, a leader in its field*
- *Has a sought after product or service*
- *Possesses top quality management*
- *Experiences steady growth*
- *Has a strong customer base*
- *Is financially strong*
- *Has low or no debt*
- *And pays a good dividend*

That's what I want my company to be.

Were I a Managing Director of a company, I would want to know that I had investors behind me not looking for quick profit but who trust me to get on with the job of building the kind of company described above. I would have

- *Pride in the company*
- *Confidence in my ability and professionalism*
- *A desire to establish the company as the best in the business*
- *And that's what I would want to be – the best in the business*

And were I an employee of a company, I would want :

- *To know that if I gave of my best that my efforts would be recognised, valued and rewarded*
- *That I had the trust of management and was seen as an important part of a team in which everyone was pulling in the same direction*

So the only difference between my 'self-employed company' and a bigger institution would be the fact that in the self-employed situation I must fulfill *all the roles* of the business – but hey! **that is quite some difference!**

It means that, not only is there no personnel other than

myself to perform the various tasks but, *crucially,* there is no other person to enforce the discipline required of me in conducting and enacting all aspects of the business. All the disciplines of work practice and of marketing and sales and of financial management and of every other of the myriad duties and activities involved in the day to day running of the business *must be imposed by myself on myself!*

POWER POINT – *"When a self-employed sales agent, all the discipline inherent in running a successful business must be rigourously self-imposed."*

So get this factor right, the need for rigourous and constant self-discipline, and you will be well on the way to a successful self-employed sales agency – *for all three of you!*

Chapter 10

TO RIVAL BRAND POPE

I have as much authority as the Pope, I just don't have as many people who believe it! - is a famous George Carlin one-liner. But like so much classic comedy the humour lies in the astute observation of, and reference to, real life. For while it's relatively easy for anyone to speak with apparent authority (just listen in at any after work happy hour), it's a different matter entirely to have people believe you!

Which of these statements, for instance, are you most likely to respond positively to : "I know what I'm speaking about, " or "Trust him his experience is valuable."

If you picked the second option then you probably did so because it is a second party recommendation and any second, or third, party recommendation is bound to carry more authority than self promotion. (Of course the person giving the recommendation must themselves be credible! Hence the desirability of multiple endorsements in the absence of any one widely acknowledged reliable authority).

And this "Trust him ..." option is worded with particular

strength. It highlights three powerful and desirable attributes ... trust, experience, value ... the inference in the recommendation being that you can depend on this individual (or company) to do what they say they will do, they know what they're doing, have done it before with integrity and excellence and will deliver a quality product or service.

So, just as you would prefer to deal with an individual or an entity reliably referred to you in this way, it is commercially wise to strive for recognition of your own sales brand by way of establishing its authority. Make your self-employed sales agency best in class and generate for yourself, your company, your product or service, enthusiastic second and third party recommendations. It might take a millennium or two to rival the authoritative status of brand Pope, but work at it. Rome wasn't built in a day!

POWER POINT – *"You are your brand. Make it known for trust, value and quality."*

Chapter 11

HOW MUCH HAVE YOU MADE TODAY?

Sales and accounts are the two departments central to the financial well-being of any business. Large or small, real world or internet, income and expenditure determine the profitability of the enterprise.

Accounts and accountants can easily identify areas of waste, 'leakage' and potential saving and can devise and implement expenditure budgets. That is their skill. But their contribution to the profitability of the business is limited within the constraints of what is available.

Sales, on the other hand, generate the 'what is available' and the potential to create income is limited only by the size of the whole market being sold into and the effectiveness in penetrating it of the sales force – in effect potential sales income is unlimited.

So it is the sales people who create the income, 'bring home the bacon' and are therefore the most prized people in the business. The super salesman is any company's most valuable asset.

So this is what you must set out to be in your business, you must prioritise your efforts on winning business. This may sound obvious but it is surprising just how many people in small businesses don't appear to realise this. They make themselves busy doing all sorts of things, anything but selling. Worse, they are often wasteful.

I myself once had a manager in my employ (not for long)! who was always ever so busy. Busy buying paper clips, coffee machines and outrageously expensive advertising in grotesque and meaningless (to our business) glossy magazines, doing anything but selling. Spending is not management, anyone can do that.

Good accounting on the other hand can and should save money on un-needed expense. And more so should focus spending on the sales department, thereby not spending at all but investing in growth.

Sales and only sales drive the business. The key question which any sales professional worth their salt will be able to answer instantly at any moment is – "How much have you made today?" This is the only meaningful indicator of sales success.

How much have you made today?

POWER POINT – *"Sales and only sales drive any business ... especially yours!"*

Chapter 12

SELLING AND BUYING

Do you notice anything odd about the above title, "Selling and Buying?" Do you perhaps think that it's a typographical error and that it should read "Buying and Selling?" That after all is the usual sequence that people would most often follow, buy something and then sell it, and therefore that's how it would normally be written – buying and selling. But no, this is no error. I have quite deliberately written Selling and Buying in that way, so the question is "Why?"

For the answer we must first go back to my observations about success and successful sales people. I have written that to 'think successful' takes a certain mindset. And, given that only a very small percentage of people are 'successful' and wealthy – 5% no more – it follows that only this select group have the 'right' attitude in this context. And their success ideas, and indeed practices, will be totally alien to what the bulk of the population thinks contributes to success.

POWER POINT – *"Learn to think like a top earning sales* *professional and accept that you will be different in attitude and action fom the bulk of other people."*

With "Selling and Buying" we have a specific example of how success orientated individuals think and act differently from anyone else. In fact, what I am about to reveal to you is one of *the single most profound 'secrets' of the super successful!* Here it is :

"Great achievers do not Buy then Sell. Great achievers only ever Sell then Buy!"

POWER POINT - *"Successful entrepreneurs never buy then sell, they first sell and then buy!"*

The simple sense of the sell then buy philosophy is so powerful that it totally goes over the head of the majority of the populace. And if presented to them most will question how it can be. Surely you must buy something before you can sell it? How can you sell something which you don't already own? Of course the answer to both of these questions is that it's perfectly possible to first sell and then to buy something but to understand the practice you must first develop the mindset and attitude of the financially super successful. Remember, very successful people generally follow very simple wealth creation practices. So simple in fact that the majority of people cannot see or will not believe that these practices are at the very heart of the their success.

POWER POINT - *"Successful entrepreneurs follow such simple wealth creation practices that the majority of people cannot see or will not believe that these practices are at the very heart of their success."*

No-one wants to or sets out to make a loss in business but what the most financially astute in society do is to ensure that the risk of loss is negligible. Therefore they develop practices which absolutely minimise the risk of loss while hugely increasing the likelihood of profit. And the Sell then Buy approach is one of their most powerful tactics. You see the Sell then Buy approach to trading gives the practitioner two huge but simple benefits. 1 – He/she need never make a loss. 2 – He/she need never hold stock.

POWER POINT - *"Sell then Buy yields two huge but simple benefits. 1 – You need never make a loss. 2 – You need never be left holding stock."*

Selling first means that a sale price is established only if it exceeds the known cost of acquiring the article and that, in turn, means that there is never any need to buy anything or to hold stock. What, after all, is the point of incurring the cost of buying, storage, staff costs and transportation when someone else will bear it? Let someone else take the risk.

By the same token it is wiser by far to work as a sales agent earning commissions rather than buy/sell stock. Better to earn $1 million in commissions and keep it all as profit rather than turn over $20 million with all the attendant hassle and cost, plus the risk, to make the same $1 million. Simple!

POWER POINT - *"Never buy anything until you have already sold it at a higher price. That way you will always make money. And when selling on a commission basis you need never buy anything!"*

So finally, and to reiterate. Never buy anything until you have already sold it at a higher price. Sell then buy. That way you **will always make money.** And working as a commission earning sales agent is a variation of the same principle!

Chapter 13

PUNISHMENT AND REWARD

As a self-employed salesman I've long practised the discipline of 'Punishment and Reward'. It's a simple and, in my view, necessary discipline if you work in sales or for yourself in any capacity.

It's no different after all than could be the case working for an employer who might, for instance, award you a bonus when you do well or might fire you for failure! So when you are your own boss it is good practice to behave likewise.

Personally I've never felt so disenchanted with my own selling performance as to feel the need to fire myself (!) but I do punish myself in other ways when I feel I've underperformed.

This might amount to denying myself a simple pleasure such as no wine with my dinner ... and with more serious failures no dinner at all! Or I might cancel time off for myself or a proposed trip abroad – yes I've done that!

On the other hand when I have a good day, close a sale, win a contract or complete a major project then I reward myself with restaurant visits, leisure breaks or foreign travel.

POWER POINT – *"The prospect of gain and the fear of pain are each powerful motivators."*

Yes, a punishment and reward policy helps to keep me focussed and motivated and to maintain a high level of performance. It's an essential part of any sales person's success strategy.

Make it a part of yours!

Chapter 14

A MERC IN THE HAND ...

Duncan's motor car of choice was a Mercedes ... and he always owned two! At every moment in time either of the near identical vehicles was available for sale. But not at any price. He sold one only when he received the premium price for it which he wanted. He was never in a hurry to sell, he sold at his leisure and for top dollar.

Only then and with cash in hand, would he set about sourcing a replacement. As with his selling, he was in no rush. He'd search for just the right car at just the right price. And the right price was bottom dollar, less in fact, it had to be a car from a seller desperate for cash, so desperate they'd let it go for peanuts. So Duncan waited. As with the sale he knew that sooner or later the right opportunity would present itself. Of course it always did.

Duncan was not only patient, he was smart. He was capitalising on two things :

Using a normally wasting asset (even Mercs lose value) in order to make profit – and he was profiting from a commodity, a necessary 'tool' which he would have in his life for business use anyway

and

The tendancy of most sellers and buyers to act in haste and based on emotion, the 'must-have-it-now' and the 'act-only-in-crisis' syndromes prevalent in much of modern society.

These two last mentioned traits go a long way to explaining why the majority of ordinary people never get to be wealthy. They are squanderers.

Duncan, on the other hand, was a predatory opportunist. He had cleverly chosen to deal in an item both necessary and of quality, one which gave him pleasure in ownership but for which he knew there was always a ready market. So his little sideline provided necessary and comfortable transport, amused and entertained him, kept him sharp and provided a dependable source of income additional to his main stream activities.

Successful sales professionals like Duncan do not become so by accident. They employ wit and wiles beyond the scope of most others. But to emulate them you need only do likewise. So are you ready to be a top earning sales professional? Do you have a Merc in the hand mentality?

POWER POINT – *"Top earning sales professionals practice being successful, it doesn't happen by accident."*

Chapter 15

NOTHING PRETENTIOUS

To strive for success, be it in some small daily activity or in a major business project, is an admirable quality. But when we achieve our goals we should never feel superior to those who have been less fortunate. Yet it happens.

The presentation was concluding with the guest speaker, a leading light in the industry and top shot salesman, inviting questions from the assembled professional delegates, some six hundred in number.

An impressionable greenhorn asked the somewhat fatuous question of him, "What kind of car do you drive?" With something of a superior upper crust drawl the toffee nose replied with the soon-to-be-his-nickname words, "Nothing pretentious, just a Bentley!" That's when I left.

I should have departed sooner, much sooner but was foolishly persuaded to extend my presence by the prospect of the free buffet and champagne to follow … yes weak and shallow I know. But while I welcome any opportunity to extend my knowledge, further my education and learn from all and sundry, I have always drawn the line at mixing with arrogant snobs. And this speaker throughout his address had made it clear to all that he looked down on the lesser beings of his audience with barely concealed contempt.

So from that day forward he became known as 'Nothing Pretentious' and he the butt of endless jokes throughout the profession. But I learned one great lesson from him.

Success at a high level in selling inevitably brings great wealth and recognition too. This places you in a position of much responsibility, where others look up to you for inspiration and guidance. So wear your success with dignity.

The simple truth is, that be you 'Nothing Pretentious' or no-one pretentious, having financial wealth makes no one person better than the next man. It doesn't make anyone important, nor does bragging about it endear them to others. In fact financial wealth is nothing.

True wealth, the wealth of the spirit and the heart, comes from friendships, generosity, love of others and the common bond of helping where-ever possible and doing so with grace and humility.

These are the ultimate riches waiting to be claimed when you set out to become a professional sales person.

POWER POINT – *"The true reward of success in selling is the opportunity it provides to help others ... wear your success with dignity and humility."*

BOOK 2

THE SIMPLEST SALES STRATEGY

How To Close The Sale Every Time!

Joseph T.Riach

Chapter 16

DO YOU WANT IMPULSE BUYERS?

I rarely if ever buy on impulse – my canny Scottish upbringing easily sees to that – and neither do I wish my clients to buy on impulse from me.

Supermarkets of course are the place where we see an appeal to impulse buy most clearly demonstrated. We all know exactly why those chocolate bars and tasty offers are placed right by the checkout. For sweets, toys or t-shirts sold to impulse in this way in major stores, there's unlikely to be difficulty should a buyer afterwards be unhappy. Brands are mostly well established ones and other items can be readily exchanged on the next supermarket visit.

But for the smaller business selling your own brand goods or services or involved in selling goods or services not in the fast-moving, light consumer goods and foods retail sectors, is promoting buying on impulse desirable? Do you want clients who haven't given due consideration to your proposal? Should you not first be intent on relationship development and building trust and reputation? You certainly can't afford to have half sold clients, or those who bought in haste, spreading negative comment.

And even if working as a commission agent or affiliate where the goods and/or services may have existing brand recognition, agents still needs to establish your own personal reputation in order to win sales ahead of fellow agents in competition and promoting the same goods/services. So in these circumstances encouraging impulse buying is neither desirable nor credible.

What is needed is a staged promotional process which first gives buyers the opportunity to establish trust in you, then your goods or service. You can still instil a sense of urgency in your call to action. But prospects must have a fair degree of certainty that they can depend on you to deliver with integrity a quality product or service which is everything you have said it will be.

So set out your stall and implement a strategy designed to develop a relationship first and a client second. Then you will find that you only ever experience a high quality brand of client, good payers satisfied with you and your offer ... and critically ... happy to recommend you to others! Leave the promotion of impulse buying to the supermarkets.

POWER POINT – *"Develop relationships first and clients second."*

Chapter 17

THE SMARTEST SMOOCHER IN TOWN

Sam wasn't a good looking lad, not by any stretch. His features were more car crash than Cruise, his physique more crisis than Christiano. In terms of intellect he was not only not at the races, he got lost on his way from the stables! And in the electric personality stakes he finished plumb last, a couple of A3s short of a flash-light beam. So what was it about him that made him irresistable to members of the opposite sex? Just what made him the smartest smoocher in town?

To say that this question persistently perplexed his teenage contemporaries of the time (myself included) is indeed an understatement. We just could not understand his success with the girls and, as time passed, his never ceasing and rapidly accumulating tally of conquests only instilled in us more and more confusion … and resentment!

That this jealousy should eventually spill over as testosteronic rage is hardly surprising in retrospect. After all it exposed the inept fumblings of the rest of us as just that, inept to the point of embarrassment. So he was duly accosted in the school yard and threatened with the proverbial duffing up behind the bike sheds if he didn't spill the beans on what he was up to ... and quick!

But when confronted and had 'the question' aggressively put to him (in terms less than complimentary) it quickly became obvious that he had not the slightest idea of what we were talking about. He was oblivious to the fact that he was cornering the market in amorous encounters like a De Beers diamond dealer and certainly had no cleverly conceived strategy which he deployed. Only at the point of imminent physical assault did he desperately stammer, "Look guys, all I do is ask!"

"What do you mean you ask?"

"Well ... er ... just that. I ask for what I want."

"You mean you just come straight out and ask a girl for ... 'what you want'?" Much guffawing from the gang ... followed by, "I'll bet you get a heck a lot of slaps on the face!" Knowing smiles and nods of agreement ... 'until ...

"Yes I do ... but I get a heck of a lot of what I want too!"

Sam you see may have lacked physical appeal or personal charisma but he possessed an inherent talent infinitely more powerful (and more powerful again because he was ignorant he possessed it)! ... Sam was smart. He accepted that there would be slap downs but understood that life delivers just what you ask of it, no more no less. No ask, no get. Simple.

Do you have it in you to be the smartest smoocher in town?

POWER POINT – *"In selling as in life ask for what you want, ask for the business!"*

Chapter 18

A TRAIN SET NAMED EMOTION

Much as I wished for it, I never in childhood became the owner of an electric train set. So handling the precision-crafted model locomotive kindled in me a nostalgia for those days long gone. I realised of course that buying the replica would not bring back those times yet, despite that, I would easily have purchased the beautiful toy had the shop assistant understood my yearning and made even a cursory effort to tap into my underlying emotion. But she didn't, she concentrated only on selling me features of the product, and her chance of a sale was gone!

The episode reminded me of the powerful sway that our emotions hold over us in buying situations.

Has anyone for example ever bought security alarms other than through fear of being victim to a break in or possible assault? Was a bed ever purchased where the buyer hadn't envisaged themselves comfortably tucked up in it? Did life insurance ever sell without a graphic scenario of bleak consequences being seeded in the buyer's mind? And what about an investment without the prospect of gain? Or would you pay a sports channel subscription fee if you expected to be bored by watching? - no, your expectation of your purchase is one of excitement and pleasure!

So be it joy, fear, greed, desire, anger, sadness or surprise, or whichever of the many other human emotions, it's necessary when on the other side of the equation as a seller to understand the need to target the emotional response of your buyer. Do this by asking questions. 'Why' is powerful, then paint word pictures or visually present real ones to ignite the buyer's dominant emotion. Highlight the benefits of your goods or services rather than the features. Appealing to emotions is everything.

I for instance don't miss the things of my youth as much as I miss my youth itself. So I did return to the shop and bought the train set. My emotional driver? Compassion for the ineptitude of the sales girl!

POWER POINT - *"People don't buy what they need, they buy what they want ... and the want is driven by emotion."*

Chapter 19

THE FAG PACK QUOTE

I have since my early years in business had (and still retain) a certain affection for what I term 'the Fag Pack Quote'. I first saw it being used many years ago by the Managing Director of a substantial, national, building services company as he spoke to a potential client on a street corner outside their offices in Glasgow. For those unfamiliar with the practice or the terminology I'll describe the scenario.

The MD and the client-to-be are engaged in an informal background chat as they walk to their cars. The prospect casually queries as to what the MD's proposed contract might in general terms cost. At that point the MD takes his packet of cigarettes (fags) from his pocket, an expensive pen from another and proceeds to do a quick calculation while scribbling the numbers on the 'fag' packet. In just a few minutes he has calculated a figure, shows it to the prospect and they shake hands on the deal! He signs off the 'quotation', gives the packet, with cigarettes(!) to the prospect and they arrange a time and place to finalise the contract. That is the 'fag pack' quote!

Of course you have to be at the top of your game, fully versed and respected in all aspects of your business and profession to have the composure and credibility to pull this off. And the fag packet could be any scrap of paper, a ticket stub, envelope, paper handkerchief or table napkin.

Now I mention this not only to enlighten and entertain you but because this method of working encapsulates a way of doing business which cuts out all the 'bull and bluster', posing, lawyers, accountants, time-wasting and cost. It is just so basic, simple and effective that you can't help but admire it – well I certainly do! And it's fun! I've practiced it myself often and still do.

Chapter 20

REPETITION REPETITION REPETITION

"And just what do you think you are doing boy!" The words boomed in my ear. I jumped, oh crikes, caught cribbing my Latin exam! The text book which I had been surreptitiously trying to consult under the desk fell to the floor (these were pre-Google days)! and the master who had crept up behind me twisted my ear and stared at me accusingly. But I was nothing if not a quick-witted little sod. Scrabbling to retrieve the fallen book I looked up and, all innocence, I chirped, "Just looking up an answer sir!" Much hilarity in the class.

Now this is where I must point out that the master in question was one of the more recent graduates to his profession and, as such, less experienced in dealing with wayward young runts given to using their intellect in directions other than those preferred by the school. He made the cardinal error of entering into a conversation – big mistake. "That's cheating," he said. "No it's not sir." "Well what is it if it's not cheating?" "It's doing what you have always taught us to do sir." "I never taught you to cheat." "No sir but you did teach us that whenever there was anything we didn't know then we should look it up and that's what I was doing!"

The soaring ego I experienced from my classmates' raucous reception to my classic punchline was instantly deflated by the beating which followed. Nursing reddened palms in the corridor outside the class from which I had been spectacularly ejected, with an imprint of the teacher's boot on my backside to prove it (he wasn't such a greenhorn after all), I pondered exactly how I was supposed to be able to write in that condition, the one hundred lines I had been assigned to complete at detention later that evening. But in the event, write them I did. One hundred times, *"O me miserum, dolor hic tibi proderit me."* I would hesitate to describe the words as my favourite Latin quote given the circumstance pertaining to my learning of them – but they are my best remembered ones! They translate as, *"Woe is me, some day this pain will be useful to me."* – and by golly that is indeed true. A good life lesson learned.

But I also learned the line – *"O me miserum, dolor hic tibi proderit me,"* rather well and, while many quotes learned and facts accumulated over time, have slipped from my recollection, that one hasn't! I have never forgotten it. And I never will. It is etched deep into my subconscious, placed there courtesy of those one hundred repetitive writings of it. Placed there by the *Power of Repetition*.

POWER POINT – *"Repetition is the single most powerful tool in creating and improving memory retention."*

It won't have escaped your notice that the title of this chapter, *Repetition Repetition Repetition*, is itself an example of …. repetition! Therefore, you should remember it because, as with anything at all that you have ever learned in your life, there is a good likelihood that some kind of repetition was involved in the process. And repetition is not only recognised as the powerful memory training tool that it is by school teachers intent on both punishing and educating their errant pupils, it is widely acknowledged and used in all areas of life.

Sporting activities are a prime example, practising a skill repetitively until it is mastered, and the world of advertising and promotion is another. Repetition is manifested daily in all kinds of media and particularly so in TV advertising. How often does the same advert appear? How many popular jingles can you recite or sing? It's no different from being that school pupil repeatedly writing the lines or others, better behaved perhaps, repeating aloud multiplication tables and other arithmetical, historical, geographical and grammatical facts and formulae. To this day they all remember their work and studies through the repetitive listening to, reading and writing down of the material. And throughout this book many points and assertions are stated repeatedly, mostly so the most salient ones such as the importance of simplicity and of ….. repetition!

In formal sales training I was taught the importance of repeating the sales message several times to prospects and clients. Early on, I often thought that such repetition was kind of insulting to the intelligence of the listener but, as any psychologist will tell you, far from it. Regardless of our level of education or intellect we all respond positively to repetition. So it's a fact, repetition works.

There's also great relevance to anyone promoting in any area of business, commerce, personal, charitable or leisure activity. Their promotional material should contain repetition. It should contain repetition in two respects :

- *Verbally - Use of words, message, expressions, slogans, terminology*

- *Visually – Lay out, theme, identity, appearance, brand*

All give the presentation a message and identity which, just like the TV jingles, audiences recognise and respond to. By using repetition there is

- *A better chance of reaching a wider audience*
- *A better chance of being noticed and remembered*

So whatever your profession or activity and whoever your target audience

- *It pays to use repetition!*
- *It pays to use repetition!*
- *It pays to use repetition!*

Chapter 21

PROFESSIONAL PROSPECT PLAN

In the early Nineties I wrote a book called 'Professional Prospect Plan'. It was aimed primarily at professional sales people. It sold well, over five thousand copies and at twenty pounds sterling each. Work out the income for yourself! Alas, not one copy survives with me. This was before the era of the internet and discs (well for me anyway) and USB sticks, and the original manuscript is long since lost in my travels. A pity, for the message which the document contained holds as good today as it did then. However, I can convey to you the gist of that message and some of the detail.

The very, very top salespeople in my industry (financial services) would typically earn at the time close to two hundred and fifty thousand pounds sterling per year. Yes, a quarter of a million! Let's say that out of that they incurred direct costs on travel, administration, telephones etc. of fifty thousand. So their net pre-tax income still amounted to two hundred thousand pounds sterling per annum. As regards their time, they would work all the hours, going the proverbial 'extra mile' striving to get to the top. And that's how they became the elite. But, typically, they would spend only one third of their working time face-to-face with prospects. The rest of their time was spent looking for clients and on administration. In other words they were not spending all their time selling. Also, they'd sell to about one third of the prospective clients who they did meet with.

My perception was (and still is) simply this. If my special skill is in selling then I want to spend all of my time doing just that – it is after all the activity which earns the income! And if I am to spend 100% of my time selling then it follows that I need support to attend to the other elements of my business. Also, I want to sell to every single prospective client with whom I meet! A tall order? Not necessarily. I calculated that my ambition could be achieved if I had the right plan. So I devised a plan and yes, *I wrote it down!* And the plan was *simple*. It was based on the premise that I'd need a team of top specialists to support my sales efforts. I decided that four people plus myself was what was required. So my team consisted of :

1. Myself – Direct Sales
2. Administrator/Personal Assistant
3. Telephonist/Sales

4. Researcher

5. Gopher/Preliminary Sales (Gopher = 'Go for this, go for that' etc.)

And this is how the system worked :

1. I drew up and specified the profile of the type of clients who I wished to deal with. This was based on my experience, knowledge of the market and on exclusive niche markets I had identified.

2. My Researcher identified by person precisely these types of prospects and compiled a full dosier on them containing all the vital information needed.

3. Administration made the initial contact with the prospect by mail.

4. Telephone Sales followed up and arranged an initial meeting.

5. My Gopher conducted this meeting and prepared the ground for my actual sales meeting with the prospect and arranged said appointment.

6. Armed with all the information garnered from each of the previous stages, I met with the client and completed the sale – an astonishing 95% of the time!

7. Administration and Gopher between them concluded all the paperwork, contracts, records and other necessary documentation and post sale contact – leaving me free to concentrate on my next sale!

Professional Prospect Plan was born!

Let's look at what I achieved in relation to the industry top earners who I referred to earlier. They, if you recall :

- Worked 'all the hours' – often 14 hours a day, 7 days per week

- Spent only one third of their time actually in front of prospective clients

- They completed a sale with one out of three such prospects

- Personally netted around two hundred thousand pounds sterling per annum – after all expenses

I on the other hand :

- Worked a 6 hour day, 3 days per week

- Spent ALL of my time in front of prospective clients

- Completed a sale 95% of the time.

- Personally netted over Two Hundred and Fifty Thousand Pounds sterling per year – after all expenses!

- Enjoyed the support of a tight and loyal team, made inclusive and rewarded well with bonuses, prizes, foreign holidays and other incentives

- Most importantly, the 'guaranteed' sales success ratio of close to 100% which the plan afforded us meant that we could enjoy our success to the full with *the luxury of working far less days and hours!* We had created great wealth but also quality time to ourselves and a real life! **More Money Less Effort!**

POWER POINT – *"With proper planning it's possible to earn far more money, expend far less time and energy and enjoy a quality personal life style too."*

And in the course of all this my success endowed me with membership of the Million Dollar Round Table in five consecutive years in the middle and late eighties.

Now I said earlier that the principles of Professional Prospect Plan hold as good today as they did then. Of course they do, and today many many professional sales people and organisations employ just this plan. *I know, I trained them.* I was employed by several major companies to enlighten their sales teams with regard to my practices. And what I taught them was my 'How I Achieved Success' strategy, in other words my Professional Prospect Plan just as outlined here.

Even in todays internet world you'll find pretty much those same practices as I've described employed by online businesses and by internet marketers all over the globe. They understand that a scatter gun approach to selling is wasteful and time consuming. They know that to achieve a high level of sales and good regular income they must thoroughly define their intended market and refine their methods of penetrating that market so as to eliminate 'tyre kickers' and identify the real prospective buyers for their goods or services. Thus they can direct all their creative energies towards the conversion of those prospects into spending customers for their offer. So technology might change but good business, and life principles, hold good.

And one of those principles is that selling is everything. It is THE most important facet of any business. Sure, all the aspects of a business must come together to form the whole but all the departments …. design, manufacture, accounts, operations, general management, technology and yes, even marketing …. important in their own ways as they are, are nothing without the sale. That's why the top salesman in a company is the only employee likely to earn more than even the C.E.O. or Managing Director. Because the ace salesperson is the guy who 'brings home the bacon'!

POWER POINT – *"The star salesman or woman is the m.v.p. (most valuable person) in any corporate team."*

However in todays modern world *it is critically important to understand* that the act of selling must be practiced as part of **a fully integrated Marketing, Sales and Customer Relationship strategy**. The tactic being to bring all these together into one synchronised unit rather than have them working separately or, as in some cases, not working at all. It is this combined approach which is efficient, effective, successful and productive – as with Professional Prospect Plan. I have dubbed the strategy as *'the Seamless Sale.'*

But you know, I've been told many times throughout my life and career by people from all kinds of backgrounds that "they don't like selling, don't like sales people" and, most significantly, "they don't want to sell and/or can't sell." Utter nonsense. Every single person on the planet sells at many points in their lives. In fact, they sell every day. Mostly they sell themselves. They do it every time they meet an acquaintance, moreso when they're introduced to a new face and, most markedly, when they set their sights on an attractive member of the opposite sex! Yup, everyone is into selling whether they realise it or not.

So it's worth remembering the following, even if your selling is restricted to just impressing that luscious lady/guy who so caught your eye last night! It was told to me as a young man by one of my millionaire mentors many years ago. It's this :

- If you have a poor product and are a poor salesperson, you'll always be poor.

- If you have a good product and are a poor salesperson, you'll still be poor

BUT

- If you have a poor product and are a good salesperson, you'll always make money …. and ….

- If you have a good product and are a good salesperson, then you'll always make lots and lots of money and be very well off

BUT

Your aim must be to sell the finest product possible and to work to be the most outstanding salesperson ever, then you'll always be very, very wealthy indeed!

Chapter 22

THE ART OF SELLING

In my business hay day, a steady stream of prospective clients would call on me daily. They'd sit before me and, almost without exception, start with the same introduction. It went like this : "Georgia Brown (or whoever) said to see you because you won't try to sell me anything." …. *" … you won't try to sell me anything … !"* Note those words. That they were repeated to me so often and with such trust remains for me to this day my proudest achievement, the finest accolade that I ever received in business or that I could ever wish to receive. You see, not only were the words they spoke absolutely spot on, I would not try to sell them anything, but as prospects said the words they would be in line of sight of a cabinet directly behind me which was groaning with silverware and major sales awards!

Does this seem like a contradiction? I'd suggest that the answer to that is both 'Yes' and 'No'. 'Yes' because all those people who visited me clearly ended off purchasing something. But 'No' because, when they consulted with me, *they were presented only with appropriate solutions, not unwanted ones, and they were given a free choice as to the course of action they preferred.* You see my view has always been that if I do the right thing for the client, as opposed to doing the most profitable thing for me, then life will do the right thing for me. And so it turned out.

POWER POINT – *"Do the right thing for other people and life will do the right thing for you."*

So when I say that the people who visited me did end up buying something, what was it they bought? Well they only ever bought one thing, and that one thing was … **me!** Actually they bought **trust in me** and the **belief that I'd do just what I said I would do!** But in reality they did not even buy those things, they didn't pay for them nor have them packaged to take away with them. So it was simply an understanding arrived at that I would provide what they wanted and they trusted me to do just that.

So, did I sell them anything at all? Actually "No" … Did I help them to find and then give them what they wanted? "Yes!" Let me explain. All the clients beating a path to my door –

- Knew that they wanted something
- Mostly did not know what that something was

- Needed someone (me) to help them identify that something

- Then the someone (me) could supply the something without selling it!

Get it? And that's what professional selling – let's call it 'not-selling' - is all about.

It's about providing - not selling - *a solution!*

POWER POINT - *"In professional selling you must win the client's trust, identify the client's wants and then supply the want – the solution."*

Thus in principle the practice of professional selling is simple. There's a sequence of actions to be followed and that sequence should be followed repetitively. And note that the words 'simple' and 'repetitive' are by far and away the two most important words to remember, not only as regards selling but with regard to all areas of life. Simple and repetitive actions add up to great achievements.

POWER POINT - *"Simple and repetitive actions add up to great achievements."*

Another extremely important point to understand about the art of selling is that good sales practices are good life practices. In other words, there is nothing that you do in successful ethical selling that you shouldn't be doing in leading a successful ethical life. Or, to put it the other way round – good life skills are good sales skills!

POWER POINT – *"Good life skills are good sales skills."*

But there's more than just that to becoming a top notch sales professional. To make the grade takes hard work (naturally), field experience and professional training and qualification. The last mentioned – studying, sitting exams and gaining professional qualifications – is all the more relevant if wishing to progress to the sophisticated selling level needed when dealing with high net worth individuals and corporations. These groups are themselves much more 'sales savy' so you have to be up for it by being prepared (done all your research, homework and training), poised (confident, ready to succeed and rehearsed for all eventualities) and persuasive (ready to state your case eloquently and deal with objections).

POWER POINT – *"To succeed in sales you must be prepared, poised and persuasive."*

When making your sales presentation … I won't call it pitch (the reason will become clear) … be it to a vast corporation or to that sexy guy/gal who has so grabbed your fancy (!), there is an infinite variety of tactics and strategies which the advanced sales practitioner can call on. But, guess what? ... most are very simple in principle and all should be used repetitively. That's not to say that it's easy to use them or to determine when, where and how or if to use them, but some basic key techniques are as follows :

- **Eye Contact :** *This is self evident ... but ...*

- **Listening :** *Is far more important than talking (hence no 'pitch')*

- **Probing :** *Gentle lead questions to establish the 'needs' (why, how)?*

- **Story Telling :** *Use real personal and 3rd party experiences to consolidate points*

- **Agreement :** *Establish common ground, likes that you share*

- **Silence :** *Creation and use of breaks in narrative is a powerful tool*

- **Take Away :** *Casting doubt on your ability to deliver increases desire*

- **Choices :** *Offer options from which client can choose course of action*

- **Confirmation :** *Confirm every point by question and*

take-away

- **Repetition** : *Repeat every point at least three times*
- **Integrity** : *Be absolutely straight, firm and honest*

One final point of extreme importance. The more you study selling (and life) skills the more apparent it should become that psychology plays a major part in pretty much everything that we say and do. If you don't come to that conclusion then you're not understanding our being at all. So it will pay you to study the subject of psychology, everyone from Freud and Jung through to modern practitioners such as John Bradshaw (Homecoming and Family Secrets) and Oliver Sacks (The Man Who Mistook His Wife For A Hat) – I heartily recommend the writings of all of these. Read them, you'll be the better for it. You will learn that, in order to understand others you must first understand yourself. Once you've got a handle on what makes you tick then you are far better placed to work out other people's behaviour. And from there you'll be able to make real progress in learning the 'fine art' of professional selling. And who knows? maybe, just maybe, one day someone will say of you, *"He won't try to sell you anything!"*

Chapter 23

SELLING MADE SIMPLE

The art of selling is little different from many other aspects of life in that it can be a complex activity or it can be a simple one. Many practitioners of sales seem to believe that complexity is not only necessary but that it is also desirable – but they couldn't be further from the truth. The truth is that simple is best and simple works.

POWER POINT – *"In selling as in every area of life, simple is best and simple works."*

So what are the simple rules of selling?

1. **Keep everything simple!** Don't over elaborate.

2. **Use repetition.** This doesn't mean that you should bombard your buyer with the exact same slogan over and over but, just like TV adverts, a message repeated is more likely to stick in the mind. But vary the way you repeat your message (eg 'the car has five doors' .. 'will you use all five doors at once?' .. 'the fifth door is the tail gate' etc.) – and then use ….

3. **Silence!** Silence is powerful, much more so than talk.

So make your point and shut up. Wait for the buyer to break the silence. When they do they will inevitably give you a ….

4. **Buying signal.** A buying signal is an expression of interest in your proposal and will most often come in the form of a question. So stay silent and wait for the question (eg 'which way does the tail gate open?') … then ….

5. **Don't answer it!** What, am I crazy? No, just smart. You see I want them to confirm the idea that is in their mind to themselves as much as to me because they themselves might not yet be aware it is there!

So when they pose their question … respond with ….

6. **Why?** The 'why' question along with silence and the 'take away' (more later) are your most powerful sales tools. When you ask 'Why'? you are demanding of your buyer that he explains exactly what it is that he wants and when he verbalises his answer it may well be the first time that he himself has realised just what it is that he actually wants (eg 'I need the tail gate to open down the way so it's like a table for picnics' – now you also know that he likes picnics, so how big a family does he have? etc.) This is why in selling it is critical not to talk facts but to ….

7. **Talk Questions and Benefits.** Puzzled? Here's an

example:

* Poor selling: Telling a fact – The car has five doors

* Better selling: Asking a question – How many doors would you like?

* Better selling: Talking benefits – With five doors you can get the whole family and all your luggage in and out easily

* **_Best selling_**: Questions and Benefits – How many doors would make life easiest for you and your family?

And when your buyer answers, then revert to ….

8. **Why?** This is in order to get validation. In other words the buyer will now use his own repetition and will repeat but with different words the reasons that he has come up with – so now he believes them himself! At this point move on to ….

9. **So if.** This is where you repeat back to the buyer what he has just said but add – 'So if … I can get you a five door etc. etc. will you buy it today?' This is called ….

10. **'Asking for the business'.** It's the one thing that many sales people find hardest to do! But it's necessary of course and at this point one of two things will happen:

a. The buyer will hesitate or say 'No'. Fine, find out 'Why'!

and start the question process again

or

b. The buyer will say 'Yes', in which case you implement the ….

11. **Take Away.** This is done to absolutely, certainly cement the sale. Any hesitation on the part of the buyer indicates that he is not ready to buy in which case you return to 'Why'? and retrace the process.

But what is the take away? It simply goes something like –

"Great, let's just make sure we've got one" *(that's take away 1)* then, " No they're all gone *(take away 2)* … will I see if we've got one down town?" *(take away 3)*.

What you're doing here is giving the buyer an opportunity to 'get out'. He could say 'No' which means that he wasn't 100% sold anyway, in which case you revert to 'Why' and proceed from there again. But you are also testing his level of interest and commitment by raising the prospect that he will not after all be able to acquire the object on which his heart is now firmly set. So when he says 'Yes' then you know that he's absolutely rock solid sold. In fact he'll be desperate to get his hands on the item. He will never change his mind and that is the only type of client that you ever want to have!

POWER POINT – *"The only kind of client you want to have are those with no doubts at all about their purchase and who will never later change their mind."*

In the example given I've only referred to the number of doors in the car. In a real sales situation each feature of the product or service would be covered in the same way as described until agreement was reached on all of them. Then finally, the major closing take away would be done on the whole product (or service).

It's a *simple* procedure and when carried out *repetitively* and well it produces outstanding results. Practice it, perfect it. It's selling made simple!

Chapter 24

THE SIMPLEST SALES STRATEGY

Of all the business, marketing and sales strategies which I have learned and applied over the years, there is one which stands out above all the rest. As with all my work practices the strategy is *simple* and in use it is of course applied *repetitively.*

The strategy actually comprises of **three elements** as follows :

1. Never try to sell anything to anyone *until they first ask you!*

2. Always follow up a request for your goods or services by *supplying something of value free!*

3. Then never supply your goods or services until *the prospect first pays you!*

In employing these three simple steps, in practice means that all your initial sales efforts are aimed not at getting the prospect to buy from you but at getting the prospect to ask you for your goods or services.

POWER POINT - *"The first and most important step in the sales process is to get the prospect to ask you to provide your goods or services."*

You see, when a prospect asks to buy then he/she feels that they are in control and are therefore bound to listen to your proposal. Thus they do not feel that they are being sold to. It's like browsing in a store. A savy sales assistant will welcome you but only to make their presence known to you eg "I'm Tom. Let me know if there's anything I can help you with." They won't try to sell you anything. But, once you have found some item of interest to you, you make the approach to the assistant and ***ask*** about it. Now you are in control and the salesperson has your permission to present appropriate benefits and solutions. And if they're half decent at their job, sale guaranteed!

So always, always direct your initial efforts at getting the prospect to ask you to provide your goods or services. Once they ask, follow up by giving them something of value free and don't conclude the sale until they first pay you. When you follow this simple three-step strategy you will find that :

- You cut out all time-wasters, as much as 90% of contacts

- You thus free up your own time to concentrate on

the 10% of genuine buyers

- You create in prospects a perception of value in your product and of professional integrity in you

- You never experience the disappointment of work done for no reward

- You create a bank of satisfied, no-hassle clients, happy to recommend you to friends and colleagues

POWER POINT - *"A prospect who first asks you and then pays you to provide your product or service becomes a happy and hassle-free client."*

So it's critically important as a salesperson to understand that, unless and until a prospect asks for your goods or services and then pays you, *you do not have a client!*

POWER POINT - *"Until a prospect first asks you for your product and then pays for it, you do not have a client!"*

In fact it gets worse. Should you attempt to sell your product or service to a prospect who did not first ask for it and latterly pay for it, it is a certainty that you will find yourself spending (read 'wasting') an inordinate amount of time and effort for no reward. In other words **high hassle, no return work.**

'Good' clients on the other hand, will have specifically

asked you to provide your goods or services and will happily have paid up front for them. These clients will by definition be *no hassle, high reward.*

Which type of client would you prefer?

Footnote : When the *"client-must-ask-and-pay"* sales strategy is added to the marketing and prospect identification practices I describe in *"Professional Prospect Plan"* and the principles and practices I describe in *"The Art of Selling"*, then you become invincible! You will have perfected **the seamless sale** where the transition from establishing your niche, to identifying your targets, to eliminating non-buyers, to completing sales is one smooth trouble-free process. You will thus be capable of selling yourself and providing a solution to just about every single prospect that you ever come in contact with. You will create far more money and from far less effort than you ever previously imagined possible. Now that's powerful!

Chapter 25

CLOSING THE SALE

The practice of closing a sale is little different from many other aspects of selling in that it can be a complex activity or it can be a simple one. Many practitioners of sales seem to believe that complexity is not only necessary but that it is also desirable – but they couldn't be further from the truth. The truth is that simple is best and simple works.

Of course the subject of closing is much studied, written of and discussed. Countless books, films and instructional guides have been published and seminars and conventions around the world regularly attract huge audiences, all clamouring to learn the secrets of 'the perfect close'. And all good professionals should indeed study and seek to learn about closing in depth. Nonetheless, it is possible to achieve outstanding results by employing very simple methods.

So following is my 'packaged', easy to understand system which can be employed in any selling environment. It is applicable to any trade or profession and can be practiced in closing the sale with regard to any goods or services and in all situations. From the simple retail sale through to complex big ticket contract negotiations ... it's a universal solution!

WHAT TO DO

This is what you must do :

THINK of closing as happening from the very opening contact with the client and carrying on right throughout the sales process. It is *not* just an isolated event occurring at the end of the sale. It is continuous throughout the process from start to finish.

In this way there is no hiatus, tension or desperation at the end of the sale because the close is already dealt with!

So how do you do this?

EMPLOY the Assumed Sale – With the assumed sale you regard the sale as a done deal (closed) right from the outset. Talk to the prospect exactly as if they are already a client. Just think of how you address an existing client and then use the same tone, words and expressions.

For example, don't use *"when"* or *"if you become a client you'll enjoy ...."*, say *"as a client you enjoy ..."* – using the present tense. No *'if'* or *'when'* but affirmative and clear. Also use *'we'* as in *"We will do well together ..."* rather than *"You might do well ..."* This positions you with the client as fellow buyer rather than opposed to him in a sales role.

Now you are on his side, empathising, jointly looking for a solution.

If in doubt as to how to proceed just study how you speak to actual clients, then do likewise with prospects. Once you've practiced this it becomes easy because you only have one manner of communication to use with all your contacts, clients or pending!

ASK questions throughout – especially 'why' and 'how' - never deliver a pitch! - listen listen, listen!

FIRST LEVEL questions might be of the "Why did you want to see me" or "What is it about ... that interests you?" or "When did you last (or ever) use ... ?"

RESPOND to answers only with a secondary question. "What makes you say that?" is a good one, or appropriate variations of that. Be sure to be genuine, concerned, interested, friendly.

REPEAT back to the client their answer to the secondary question but using different words and ...

ASK for the client's confirmation that you have understood their response eg "So what you are saying is ... ?"

LISTEN to their response and follow up with a third level question.

THIRD LEVEL questions are critical. They relate to the client's feelings, their emotions eg "Why do you feel that?" or "How does that make you feel?" or "What does that mean to you?"

What you have done up to now is :

FIRST level 'whys' and 'hows' tell you *facts* about the client.

SECOND level questions expose their *needs* or *wants*.

THIRD level questions identify their *dominant buying motive*, their underlying *emotional* trigger. It could for example be 'concern' for a loved one, 'desire' for something they don't have or the 'fear' of loss of something they already have!

So time to ...

APPLY a Minor Decision close – This is where you ask the client *"Will we ... "* to decide on a minor point of the product or service as opposed to them saying yes to the whole deal. Just ask for a simple preference choice on the one particular point you are at the stage of discussing. eg "Will we go for red or blue?" or "Will we put your wife on the policy too?" By agreeing to that or not the client is giving permission to move forward. So now confirm their decision by way of a ...

TAKE AWAY – which is a way of putting the client at ease, of testing their commitment, giving them a chance to back off – and increasing their desire! So it's an essential and powerful step!

A 'take away' could be, "You are sure about that?" or "I'll just check we can do that" or, very powerful, "Of course this may not be for you." But the thing is to make certain that you have their agreement, that this point is without doubt 'closed'. Only when certain move on to ...

Asking for **PERMISSION** to move on. This is the last essential step of closing the point you have been discussing. It's kind of like a second take away and confirms the client as being in control, of deciding what's happening eg "So we're doing the red/the wife on policy, yea? Okay can we look at ... now?"

And only when permission is granted then move on to the next point, and the next one and so on, until you've covered everything.

WHEN you arrive at the very last point in the whole presentation, deal with it and close it in the same way too.

THIS last minor point close thereby becomes the close on the whole deal! But the body of the sale is already, stage by stage, long since agreed to and closed.

And as you have been assuming the business to be a done deal from the word go then the client has too. So move smoothly to wrap up the meeting. Where payment is involved ask if it's cheque, cash, card or app (minor decision close) and/or simply offer a handshake and tell them what they can expect to happen next.

My preference at the conclusion was usually to take my pen out (always a good quality one) and say, "Your name, is that spelled with an 'm' or an 'n'?", or whatever (minor decision close) and start writing. But even at simple retail level you've experienced the classic, "Do you want it gift wrapped?" line. So you see it's all around and it works!

What you have done in this sales process described is employed four key sales skills :

Gathering information

Responding to information

Delivering information

Asking for something or Closing

From the outset you haven't tried to sell anything. You

have :

Questioned to find the client's need

Listened and requestioned to establish their want (different from need) and the all important emotional connection

then

Suggested a solution and requested permission to supply it!

So by employing this approach to closing a sale you eliminate, both for yourself and the client, all the stress often associated with the round-off of the selling process. And with its use it is perfectly possible to enjoy successful closing experiences throughout an entire sales career ... and with no real need to understand the process in greater depth. After all, many of the more advanced closing techniques are already built into the system!

So concentrate only on providing a rewarding and enlightening experience for your client. Listen intently, question and encourage the client to do the talking. Then the closing will look after itself.

POWER POINT – *"Assume that the client is sold/closed from the word go!"*

HOW TO EMPLOY THE CLOSE

Following is a real example of all the afore-mentioned in action - This is my actual intro used over many years ׃

Me ׃ Hi I'm Joseph Riach, just call me Tom all my friends do.

I've assumed the client to be my friend plus planted a question for him which immediately brings him in on a personal level.

Client ׃ How come they call you Tom?

Me ׃ Well I was christened Joseph Thomas Riach the same as my dad. He was called Joe in the household so I became Tom ... and it stuck. It meant that we didn't both rush at the same time when mum called 'cos one of us was in trouble!"

I've introduced a story (good practice) and some light humour.

Client ׃ So Tom it is. I'm Bill.

Me ׃ That's short for William of course? Was it your dad's name too or was it passed down from someone else in the family?

This is first level why, how question. Putting client at ease by getting him talking about himself. Time to listen!

Client now gives me a bit of a run down on name, family etc. aided by occasional prompts from me ... then ...

Me : So you never actually knew your grandfather?

Second level question.

Client : No, he survived the war but afterwards didn't want contact with anybody.

Me : How did that make you feel?

Bang! Third level question.

Client then describes some of his emotions both at the time and now.

Me : So if you had the same situation face you now would you deal with it as you did or do something different?

Empathising with client and giving a minor decision close.

Client answers.

Me : You don't sound entirely sure about that?

Take away.

Client responds.

Me : We all have to live with these kinds of things Bill but we can't let it effect our present business, can we?

Empathising with client, assuming the sale and asking for permission to move on.

Client : Certainly not. So what have you got for me?

Point closed and permission granted to move on to next point

Me : Something your grandfather would just love Bill! ... but tell me first, what is it about ... that caught your attention?

Tapping into the previous emotion, adding suspense ... and back to first level question and on to the next point ...

... and the next one and so on, until every point is covered and closed. in the same way.

Deal done!

So think of the sales process as a long country lane. It has high walls on either side and you must progress from the opening exchanges at one end of the alleyway to the 'close of the deal' at the other end. From start to finish there is a series of open gates representing the various stages of the relationship which you are developing with your client. As you pass through each gate it must be firmly closed behind you so that the only way forward for you and your client is to go on to the next gate. You cannot move on to the next gate until the previous gate is closed. And then the next, and the next and so on until the process is complete. No one gate is any more or less important than any other because it as all the gates collectively which represent the close and any one gate not firmly closed will allow your client to backtrack and your momentum willl be lost, you will not get to the end of the lane – and the ultimate completion of your deal.

A REAL-LIFE SCENARIO

Now here is a real-life scenario which demonstrates the assumed sale and close in action. I have employed many variations of this over the years but the key elements and general approach never vary :

The six in the morning glint in farmer Sandy Duncan's eye was induced little by the watery, winter sun rising over the Grampian hills but much by the mischief occupying his mind. Thumbs entrenched in classic rural manner around the bib of his mucky dungarees and chewing on unlit clay pipe, he was leaning by the gate of his 'bottom field'; that rough tangle of gorse and weed farthest from the farmhouse, lowest down by the stream and a veritable bog of sodden misery lieing in wait for the unwary.

He turned his eye to the mud, gravel and pot-hole mosaic of track lurching upward from his lolling point and scanned narrow-eyed for his prey. A thin smile glanced his lips. His intended victim was to be yet another 'pretentious, pinstripe-suited, city slicker' lured at unholy hour to this ungodly spot by Sandy's vague insinuation of 'lucrative business to be had', only for him and his smart limousine to be waylayed in the stinking myre of Sandy's midden and sent empty-handed on his way, a muddied and humiliated, soaking mess.

But as Sandy caught sight of an old and battered Land Rover weaving its way along the lane towards him, his eyebrows furrowed, the image of his perfect ambush wilted somewhat and his pipe sagged in his lips. What was this?

I pulled the Land Rover to a halt with a squelch and not unimpressive slither, smack in front of Sandy, threw open the door and jumped out. He was crestfallen to see that I wore knee-high wellington boots, denim jeans and a tatty Barbour jacket. Before he could say a word I fearlessly grabbed his sharn-spattered hand, shook it vigourously and proclaimed, "Good morning Mr.Duncan, this is quite some place you've got here. I'm told you have the finest beasts (cattle) in the glen. Can we go see them now?!" A canny pause while he scrutinized me thoughtfully, then a drawn out, "Aye, we can that."

Twenty minutes and a soggy sludge through the fields later we were close up and personal with his prize herd in the byre (cow-shed) and he was introducing me enthusiastically and in detail to each and every one of them. Bang! - Deal closed! Yet not a word of any potential business of any kind has been mentioned or discussed. We have only just met.

The rest of the day passed with Sandy proudly showing me around the entire farm and concluded seated by the massive open range fire in the kitchen, his wife Janet prodding me with queries of my life and treating me to her freshly baked scones; my genuine and enthusiastic approval of which dealt conclusively with any possibility of opposition to any business proposal from that quarter.

The next time I visited Sandy, he and his wife welcomed me glowingly at the door of their farmhouse. The day passed with heaped servings of Mrs.Duncan's hot girdle scones, mugs of farmyard tea and hilarious tales of city business executives whose pride, sanity and Armani suits Sandy had gleefully sabotaged during early morning rendez-vous in his bottom field.

Only as I was leaving did Sandy ask for the first time about 'business'. We exchanged a few words, agreed a course of action and shook hands.

And that ... is how to close a deal!

A LOOK AT THE PSYCHOLOGY

Let's look at the psychology inherent in the above scenario and the elements of good relationship building (not selling) technique employed. How many can you spot?

Preparation : I had done my homework, reconnoitered the farm premise previously, learned about the prospect, who he was, his character and preferences and knew what to expect. In this way and with every point mentioned below I was from the word go 'closing the gates'!

Appearance : I dressed for success, appropriate to the client and to the situation.

Transport : I arrived as one familiar with the territory and therefore au fait with life in the region, requirements and local custom.

Language : I adopted country language but showed respect too.

Control : I took control of the situation from the off and assumed the sale.

Interest : I showed an immediate and genuine interest,

knowledge and no fear of the subject closest to the prospect's heart, his beasts. *I got straight to his emotional hot spot!*

Questions : I asked first level questions then listened as he spoke.

Rapport : All of this is about quickly establishing my identity, establishing common ground and building trust.

Information : I never mentioned business but spoke openly about myself when prompted in order to satisfy his wife's natural curiosity and put them at ease with me.

Compliments : I paid genuine compliments regarding his reputation, beasts, farm and his wife's baking!

Business : I made no reference to business until he asked! Only then did I do a brief 'fag pack' close. Deal done!

You see with my whole approach I put myself immediately 'onside' with my client as a friend to be trusted, not an outsider, adversary or one to be feared. He never felt threatened, undermined nor sold to!

So, if you are already, or intend to become, a sales person or marketer of any kind or if you simply want to upgrade your communication skills and be a better person then this is all it takes. It's not hard, very simple in fact. But it will be necessary for you to re-evaluate how you perceive selling and the sales process and go to school on it.

Remember that the most effective selling is 'non-selling', it is all about empathy and trust. The 'seamless sale' is a total marketing, selling and customer relationship exercise. It is a joyful and fun experience for all involved. If you don't 'get that' and all that I've just disclosed, then I urge you to redouble your study – that or give serious thought to employing your talents in some other profession or discipline.

Chapter 26

THE CREDIBILITY FACTOR

A client will not do business with a sales person who they find to be incredible, that's as in not believable. And the surest way to plant doubt in the mind of your client about your credibility is to talk too much. Somewhere in everyone's psyche is an image of the fast-talking, foot-in-door 'barrow boy', delivering a hectic pitch of how great their product is and how lucky the client is to have him there to put things to right.

The reality is that clients relate to a salesperson who takes the time to listen to them and find out what's important to them. Nobody is bored or turned off when they are talking. They are bored when you are talking!

So rein in your ego and know to show humility. Don't overstate the benefits of your goods or services (over selling), rather tell your client what it can't do (a take away) so that they'll better believe what it will do! Then shut up and wait for them to ask a question. This will come as a buying signal so don't be afraid to tough out the silence. This is what top sales people are masters at, they don't fear losing the sale by keeping quiet. They assume all sales situations as done deals from the word go, all prospects as being clients. So their focus is entirely on winning. They look ahead, plan ahead and take risks when necessary.

This attitude reflects back on the client. They subconsciously lock on to it and become part of the process. They respond to the emotional prompts in your questions and you'll know when you have established credibility with them when, having disclosed to you some private or intimate detail about themselves or their situation, they say "I don't know why I told you that!", or something similar. They told you because they trust you!

I have always said that I know more about many of my clients than do their spouses or partners. Why do they tell me so much? Because I prompt with gentle questions sympathetic to their emotions. So they grow to know that they can trust me, rely on my discretion and that I'll never in any circumstance repeat anything they tell me. After all, they never hear me talk of or disclose information about other clients.

They do however hear me accept responsibility for the success or otherwise of our professional relationship.

So just as an over-inflated ego and too much blarney on

your part will certainly kill any prospect of a sale, credibility established in you by your displaying of a caring and emotional persona, one prepared to listen and empathise, will guarantee successful conclusions for both you and your client – every time.

THE MOTIVATION TO GET YOU TO YES

IMPOSSIBLE CONVERSATIONS

In signing off on my Simplest Sales Strategy, I am repeating many important points, emphasising some others and making further observations too – all designed to help you further grasp the key elements of the selling process and the simple psychology involved.

We live in a time when much is said about stress and stress-related illness. Difficult situations certainly exist for many people but my belief is that most modern day stress is self-induced. This being so, then the answer to enjoying a stress free life lies in your own hands. It takes courage and it takes action but a sublime life, one free of unhealthy pressures or worry, awaits all those of you prepared to take control of your own future. The majority of successful sales people do just that.

The day that I realised that selling was necessary in order to progress in life, and that it is nothing more than listening then acting accordingly, was the day that any concerns in life I may have had disappeared and my career took off. I literally rocketed into the stratosphere businesswise and all I did was change emphasis from pushing to listening! It was a veritable 'Ah-ha!' moment - like the flick of a lightswitch and the accompanying brilliance following it!

At the same time I learned to under-sell in promotion in order to over-perform at the point of delivery; thereby exceeding clients' expectations and creating friends for life! And under-selling demands listening more so than active promotional skills.

You may well have heard it said, "I don't like selling. I don't like sales people. I don't like being sold to." You may even have pronounced it yourself. But why? I believe there are two inter-related answers. The first is that the statements reveal a lack of self-confidence in the speaker. The second is that they show a lack of understanding of what selling is.

So, what is selling? Answer – it is a life skill. As such it is an activity which all humans (and many animal species) practice regularly. Some are better at it than others, but all humans sell. The most obvious regular example is in attracting a mate. Everyone goes into 'sell mode' when that is on the agenda! Those who work at improving their skill in this department, improve their chances of 'catching the gal or the guy'. So why not apply it to other areas of life as well?

The Simplest Sales Strategy

There persists among many the common misconception that selling is somehow 'unworthy', that it's carried out by stereotypical, fast-talking, foot-in-door, 'wide boy', market traders as often depicted in popular comedy; but that is not selling. Real professional selling is all about communication.

Let's replace 'selling' in the opening prejudiced lines with the word 'communication' and see how that alters the whole slant of the statement :

"I don't like communication. I don't like communicators. I don't like being communicated with." Sounds a bit narrow-minded doesn't it? And 'silly' too. Yet that is what "I don't like selling ... " amounts to. It's not a very well thought through statement when viewed in that light. Communication, rather than implying some sort of one-sided, brow-beating exercise, is, by definition, a two way relationship. There is talking and there is listening. Good communicators listen more than they talk and that is the paramount skill of an accomplished sales person – listening.

Let's cement the point further by replacing 'selling' in the opening lines with the word 'listening' :

"I don't like listening. I don't like listeners. I don't like being listened to!" It gets ridiculous doesn't it? While there are shouty, virtue-signaller types and selfish boors who don't want to listen and have no intention of doing so, it's improbable that you have come across, or are ever likey to encounter, anyone who objects to being listened to. On the contrary, being listened to is what most people crave. A life-skilled, professional sales person satisfies that craving. They listen, they empathise.

In everyday life you too can do likewise. For, "I don't like selling," substitute, "I do like listening!" It really is that simple. A case of ... Listen, if you want to know a secret!

Unfortunately, I believe that among the general population people's listening, debating, discussing and simple arguing skills are in decline. This is because there is more polarisation in society than before. Conversations on contentious issues held in good faith seem to be vanishingly rare. Debate on a whole manner of issues seems to have given way to nothing more than denunciations of 'the other side'. Driven by social media people just 'go with the tribe' and dig in to the headline emotion of the day rather than researching, thinking through and establishing their own reasoned views. Such folk are hard to communicate with freely and therefore more difficult to sell an alternative idea or solution to.

To overcome these hurdles, any person wishing to share

meaningful discussion with others, and this includes professional sales people, need to have a greater grasp of communication, conversation and listening skills than ever before. This includes an understanding of how the spread of identity divides have adversely affected the way people communicate because identity divides have certainly made conversation more difficult.

Sociologists talk about a concept called 'competitive victimhood'. Essentially what happens is, once one group starts playing identity division through claims to victimhood and by using offence-taking as a political tool, then you'll see other groups starting to play the same game and creating their own victimhood narratives.

There are three layers of difficulty as regards open conversation.

The first, and easiest to negotiate, are fact-related discussions. Second, and more problematic, are those where emotions are involved. Conversations relating to the third level, identity matters, are however by far the ones most difficult to negotiate. Once identity comes into the picture, conversation can become almost impossible.

Identity related conversations are characterised by participants who refuse to budge from a pre-set viewpoint and literally freak out when challenged. Such types may not even concede that the only way to resolve situations is by having a conversation. They choose instead to 'be offended' by opposing beliefs and like to shut down dialogue as in, "I don't like sales people." I find the idea that you wouldn't want to talk to somebody to be somehow deeply tragic. It robs the proponents themselves of an opportunity to challenge and question their own beliefs and to become more humble about what it is that they think they know.

So, whether a professional sales person or just someone intent on developing your life skill of communication, you need to give consideration as to how you can communicate in the most demanding of circumstances, how you can negotiate even 'impossible conversations'.

But, before you even talk about impossible conversations, you have to go back to just conversations. You have to think about what is the goal of a conversation. Why are you in the conversation? And are you really listening and understanding?

The first 'rule' in any conversation is to never start by attacking another person's idea. Rather be sure to understand it intimately, to the extent that you can express it even more clearly than they can! If you only know your own side of the argument, then you know little of that. Make the other party want to say, "Oh, I wish I had thought of that", and mention things you have learnt from them, too. It is easy to run around spouting conclusions, but very few people talk about how they came to their conclusions – 'how you know what you think you know'. So organise your conversations around questions, not topics. Ask targeted questions. Ask people how they know what they think they know! That gets you up to moderately difficult conversations.

It is a good strategy to introduce scales into questions. Scales are incredibly powerful tools. You ask, for example, "On a scale from one to ten, how confident are you in the truth of what you just told me?" This enables you to understand how firmly someone believes something. This avoids conversations devolving into, "Yes, we do" or "No, we don't," responses. Ask the person you are in conversation with to rate their belief on a scale and then ask them to rate an alternative belief in the same way. Now you can better situate their belief. And use the simple confirmation questions. eg "Under what conditions could that belief be false?"

But you need a whole new skill set for impossible

conversations – where the gulf is seemingly unbridgeable. This is when you ask how confident another person is in a belief on a scale of one to ten and they answer, "Eleven!" You'll get nowhere with these types until you start having good regular conversations. You can't just jump into the impossible. You have to start at the basic level and then move your way forward. Success is really in terms of just being able to have the conversations – not so much a case of changing people's minds as opening their minds to hear from another perspective. For instance, lead them to realise that – "He is a salesman but he's a good guy and I can listen to him and take his ideas more seriously". That's actually nine-tenths of the battle. If your goal is to overcome someone's resistance, then commit yourself not to just one conversation but to a series of conversations. These things take time.

Identity divides do not, however, move easily. Usually, people have lots of defences to prevent that. When you have a conversation around identity or that has identity-level salience, you really have to affirm the other person's identity. If they feel like their identity is under threat, they are not going to get past that point. Similarly, in an 'emotional' conversation, you have to acknowledge that the other party are justified in feeling whatever emotion they feel, even if that emotion is not productive. There has to be a level of acknowledgement and recognition.

If you can't begin by acknowledging and affirming that their intentions are honourable and if you can't phrase what you're doing in terms of recognising those moral intuitions and appealing to them, you'll have a hard time reaching them. Loyalty is often important to them. So try to appeal to those kinds of things when making your case. Learning to speak in another person's moral language is an important, albeit a very difficult, component.

Bear in mind that the people who have these moral impulses or intuitions about things, often don't know how to actually respond properly. They just call people names. They don't have the moral infrastructure to deal with the issues because they've never heard opposing arguments to them. So they make no attempt to engage other than in a hostile way. The conversation goes nowhere.

This kind of dire, non-interaction comes up a lot – but it needn't. A fundamental rule of thumb is if somebody feels like you're not listening to them, they're not going to listen back. You aren't going to be able to convince somebody of your view if they don't feel heard. A surprising number of the techniques in this book can be boiled down to listening and listening well.

I may talk a lot about listening … but I listen to a lot of talk too!

POWER POINTS OF SELLING

The Power Points of Selling highlighted throughout this book form rules or mottoes to be followed determinedly and to live your life and conduct your sales business by. As such they are critical to your success. Read them, memorise them, employ them. You'll be the better for it.

This section is both a reminder and a quick reference of those and I've also added a selection of some of my other favourite motivational 'bites' to inspire and guide you.

"Those who wish to become successful and wealthy and achieve great things must think and act totally differently from the rest of the population."

"Top sales professionals create their own fortune from their own efforts."

"When you set out to achieve great things the only risk you take is the risk of success."

"When you take full control of your situation and assume full responsibility for all of your actions, success becomes a virtual certainty."

"Learn to think like the wealthy 5% of the population and accept that you will be different from 'Joe Public'."

"Simple activities carried out repetitively and well are what mount up to great achievements."

"Learning to act simply will not be easy. Be prepared to uneducate yourself from thinking and working in complex ways."

"The majority of the population display by all their thoughts and actions a desperate desire to be equal in mediocrity."

"Winners are mentally tough, strike early and choose their moments well."

"The world of selling is tough and competitive, demanding effort and dedication. Only the most resolute prevail."

"There is nothing that you do in life which you won't do better by being physically fit."

"When you exercise your body, you exercise your mind and vice versa. It's win-win!"

"Simple activities carried out repetitively and well are what mount up to great achievements."

"You sprint for show but you jog for dough!"

"A constant learner is a constant earner!"

"Top sales people are questioners and listeners – not talkers."

"Asking 'stupid' questions is smarter by far than not knowing."

"Negative thoughts become negative words become negative actions. Eradicate from your mind all reference to them."

"The ability of leading sales professionals to be self-critical is one of their great strengths. When questioning events affecting them they look first, in the mirror."

"When you take it upon yourself to be responsible for yourself, for your life and for your situation then you take the first step to achieving great things."

"Whenever you have an idea or an ambition to really achieve something then you must start by putting it down in writing."

"Turning an idea into a written plan is the first necessary step to make in progressing from just an idea in your mind to implementation."

"Before writing your sales business plan, start by writing down your 'I Want' list of material objects and lifestyle requirements which the venture is intended to create for you."

"Take control of your own destiny and accept responsibility for all that happens to you by becoming your own boss."

"You must become your own boss and write down your business plan based on your 'I Want' list."

"When a self-employed sales agent, all the discipline inherent in running a successful business must be rigourously self-imposed."

"You are your brand. Make it known for trust, value and quality."

"Sales and only sales drive any business, especially yours!"

"Learn to think like a top earning sales professional and accept that you will be different in attitude and action fom the bulk of other people."

"Successful entrepreneurs never buy then sell, they first sell and then buy!"

"Sell then Buy yields two huge but simple benefits – You

need never make a loss and need never be left holding stock."

"Never buy anything until you have already sold it at a higher price. That way you will always make money. And when selling on a commission basis you need never buy anything!"

"The prospect of gain and the fear of pain are each powerful motivators."

"Top earning sales professionals practice being successful, it doesn't happen by accident."

"The true reward of success in selling is the opportunity it provides to help others ... wear your success with dignity and humility."

"Develop relationships first and clients second."

"In selling as in life ask for what you want, ask for the business!"

"People don't buy what they need, they buy what they want ... and the want is driven by emotion."

"Repetition is the single most powerful tool in creating and improving memory retention."

"With proper planning it's possible to earn far more

money, expend far less time and energy and enjoy a quality personal life style too."

"The star salesman or woman is the m.v.p. (most valuable person) in any corporate team."

"Your aim must be to sell the finest product possible and to work to be the most outstanding salesperson ever, then you'll always be very very wealthy indeed!"

"Do the right thing for other people and life will do the right thing for you."

"In professional selling you must win the client's trust, identify the client's needss and then supply their want – the solution."

"Simple and repetitive actions add up to great achievements."

"Good life skills are good sales skills."

"To succeed in sales you must be prepared, poised and persuasive."

"In selling as in every area of life, simple is best and simple works."

"The only kind of client you want to have are those with no doubts at all about their purchase and who will never

later change their mind."

"The first and most important step in the sales process is to get the prospect to ask you to provide your goods or services."

"A prospect who first asks you and then pays you to provide your product or service will be a happy and hassle-free client."

"Until a prospect first asks you for your product and then pays for it, you do not have a client!"

"Assume that the client is sold/closed from the word go!"

"The secret of success is ... to live happily!"

"Are you prepared to take the risk of becoming successful?"

A WORD FROM THE AUTHOR

It's an old adage but a good one ... *Save the best 'til last!* And that's just what I've done ......

Whenever you set out to achieve great things, to become successful whether materially or spiritually, you have to take a risk. The risk you take however is simply the risk of being successful. So be bold! *Expose yourself to the risk of success!*

But be prepared to receive an abundance of negative comment and adverse criticism. Your efforts will be sneered at. Never mind, pay no heed. Your critics, smug in their mediocrity, will never have taken a risk in their lives. They will never have exposed themselves to the risk of success and will certainly never have experienced it. Therefore their opinions are totally worthless. Ignore the hollow comment of the non-trier, non-doer and the non-achiever.

At the beginning of my career I set out with the aim of creating monetary wealth and becoming successful. But although I worked tirelessly I achieved little of either. However, over time, through experience and with the counsel of those older and far wiser than myself, I learned that the sure route to unlimited wealth lay in working on improving my sales skills.

But more so ... that the *secret* to success in selling lay in concentrating all of my efforts in helping others.

So that is what I did. I focused purely on helping others. And it is from that strategy that my successful career in sales flowed.

But the question arose as to how many others could I, should I help? Answer – as many as possible. But is that hundreds, thousands or even millions? I was perplexed. Then I remembered a conversation I had had with a friend many years previously. The friend had been dismissive of my pursuit of wealth and its trappings, expressing instead their desire to save endangered species, the tiger in particular. In response to this I had posed the question, "How many?" My point being that to save the beautiful creatures would take the very money which my friend so despised ... and lots of it! My friend's response 'though was simple and clear – "I want to save them all."

So that became my starting point too and to this day remains my goal ... I want to *help everyone!*

And this is the most important success in sales principle

which I have to pass on to you.

Whatever you want from life, the best way to get it is to *focus your energy in helping others.*

- *If you want higher self-esteem then find ways to boost someone else's self-esteem.*

- *If you want to raise your positive spirit then assist someone else to raise theirs.*

- *If you want more success the smartest way to get it is to help someone else achieve it.*

- *And if you want more money from more sales – first help others to get what they want!*

When you give generously of your time and effort in these ways then in due course you will discover as if by magic that the biggest beneficiary of your efforts is .. you! You'll first become spiritually rich, relaxed, confident and inwardly calm. Then be assured, the material wealth will follow.

Joseph Tom Riach

RESOURCES

Not all the resources listed are referred to directly in this book. But all are valuable sources of inspiration and motivation which have proved to be of immense value to me, my students, sales professionals and others.

Literature

Annapurna South Face – *Sir Chris Bonington*

Family Secrets – *John Bradshaw*

Homecoming – *John Bradshaw*

Mastering the Art of Making Money – *Joseph T.Riach*

Self Improvement Should Be Fun! – *Joseph T.Riach*

The Collected Works of Carl Jung – *Carl Jung*

The Complete Psychological Works of Sigmund Freud – *Sigmund Freud*

The James Bond Novels – *Ian Fleming*

The Man Who Mistook His Wife For A Hat – *Oliver Sacks*

The True Story of the First Ascent of Everest – *Sir Edmund Hilary*

The Works of Lord Byron – *Lord Byron*

Winning Big In Life And Business – *Joseph T.Riach*

Online

Author's Press Releases – *Joseph T.Riach, ibosocial.com/wakeup2wealth*

Author's Web Site – *www.tomriach.com*

Films

Chariots of Fire – *Producer David Puttnam, Writer Colin Welland, Director Hugh Hudson. Academy Award Best Film 1981*

The Great Dictator – *Written, directed, produced, scored by and starring Charlie Chaplin. Nominated for five Academy Awards 1940*

Quotes

"If at first you don't succeed ... try, try, try again" – *William E.Hickson (often erroneously attributed to Robert the Bruce, King of Scotland 1306-1329)*

"Speak up for yourself ... and then always be true to your word" – *my mother*

"Nothing in the world can take the place of persistence ... " – *Ray Kroc*

"Pick Yourself Up .. Start All Over Again" – *Dorothy Fields (music by Jerome Kern)*

"It is not the critic who counts ..." – *Theodor Roosevelt, U.S.President*

"Keep right on to the end of the road ... " – *Sir Harry Lauder*

"This is no time to make new enemies ..." – *Voltaire*

Sources of Inspiration

Warren Buffet – *Investment professional, often ranked the world's richest man*

Richard Branson – *Millionaire entrepreneur and adventurer*

Andrew Carnegie – *Steel magnate, industrialist and philanthropist*

Walt Disney – *Cartoonist and film maker*

Ralph Lauren – *Fashion designer*

Steve Jobs – *Founder of Apple Inc.*

Henry Ford – *Automobile manufacturer*

J.K.Rowling – *Author*

Samuel Walton – *Retailer*

Harry Barclay – *Scottish farmer and businessman*

Oprah Winfrey – *Television presenter, often ranked as the world's richest woman*

Seve Ballesteros – *Professional golfer*

Charles Chaplin – *Film actor, director and comic genius*

Bob Dylan – *Singer/song writer*

The Beatles – *Worldwide success phenomenon*

Other

Aberdeen Grammar School – *One of oldest schools in UK, founded 1257*

Wake Up – *The author's leisure and learning breaks, personal mentoring and business guidance courses which he conducts in the sunny south of Portugal. See www.ibosocial.com/wakeup2wealth*

COPYRIGHT AND DISCLAIMER

The Simplest Sales Strategy

The life of which you dream is here within your grasp!

ISBN : 978-1540678041

© **Joseph T.Riach 1998 - 2019 all rights reserved**

All proprietory rights and interest in this publication shall be vested in Joseph T.Riach and all other rights including, but without limitation, patent, registered design, copyright, trademark and service mark, connected with this publication shall also be vested in Joseph T.Riach.

No part of this publication may be reproduced, stored in a retrieval system, or transmitted in any form or by any means, electronic, mechanical, photocopying, recording or otherwise, without the prior written permission of the copyright owner, Joseph T.Riach.

The right of Joseph T.Riach to be identified as the author of this work has been asserted in accordance with the Copyright, Designs and Patents Act 1988.

Designations used by companies to distinguish their products are often claimed as trademarks. All brand names and product names used in this book are trade names, service marks, trademarks or registered trademarks of their respective owners. The publisher is not associated with any product or vendor mentioned in this book.

Limit of liability/disclaimer of warranty. While the publisher and author have used their best efforts in preparing this book, they make no representations or warranties with respect to the accuracy or completeness of the contents of this book and specifically disclaim any implied warranties of merchantability or fitness for a particular purpose. It is sold on the understanding that the publisher is not engaged in rendering professional services and neither the publisher nor the author shall be liable for damages arising herefrom. If professional advice or other expert assistance is required, the services of a competent professional should be sought. This manuscript relates only the personal experience of the author.

The Simplest Sales Strategy is available direct from the Amazon book store (amazon.com or amazon.co.uk) in Paperback and Ebook formats, Barnes and Noble and other leading book suppliers.

Receive notifications of my new books and novels as they become available, free and reduced price book offers and entry to periodic promotions for signed or personalised copies of my books, by visiting me at tomriach.com, clicking 'Contact' and leaving a message.

Also, to help ensure that I can continue to create quality publications at affordable prices, I would really appreciate a review on Amazon. The number of reviews a book receives on a daily basis has a direct impact on how it sells, so just leaving a review, no matter how short, helps make it possible for me to continue writing books for you to enjoy. To see a selection of the many reviews sent directly to me, but not featured on Amazon, visit my website at tomriach.com and click 'Reviews'.

Thanking you for reading my work and for your ongoing support.

Author's Amazon Pages – *Joseph T.Riach,*
https://www.amazon.com/-/e/B01MTQYSH3
https://www.amazon.co.uk/-/e/B01MTQYSH3

Author's Leisure And Learning Breaks In Portugal –
https://www.ibotoolbox.com/wakeup2wealth/pressrelease.aspx?prid=197923#

Author's Press Releases – *Joseph T.Riach,*
https://www.ibotoolbox.com/wakeup2wealth/pressrelease.aspx

Author's Web Site – *http://www.tomriach.com*

www.ingramcontent.com/pod-product-compliance
Lightning Source LLC
Chambersburg PA
CBHW061438180526
45170CB00004B/1466